LEONID PLYUSHCH was an engineer-mathematician at the Cybernetics Institute of the Ukrainian Academy of Sciences in Kiev. In 1968, at the age of twenty-nine, he wrote an open letter to *Komsomolskaya Pravda*, challenging the truth of its report of the Ginzburg-Galanskov trial. Shortly afterwards he was dismissed from his post at the Institute. In 1969, with fourteen others calling themselves an Initiative Group for the Defence of Civil Rights in the USSR, he signed an appeal to the UN, listing numerous Soviet trials since 1966 as violations of human rights. He participated in similar appeals in 1970.

In January 1972 Plyushch was arrested during an extensive round-up of Ukrainian intellectuals. He spent a year under investigation by the KGB, and a team of forensic psychiatrists of the Serbsky Institute, Moscow, declared him of unsound mind. In January 1973 he was tried, *in absentia* and *in camera* (both specific violations of the Soviet legal procedural code) and sentenced to compulsory treatment in a special psychiatric hospital. After futile appellate procedures, he was finally confined in the Dnepropetrovsk special psychiatric hospital and subjected to massive doses of haloperidol, followed by increasing doses of insulin (he is not a diabetic) and, more recently, heavy doses of 'triftazin', an anti-schizophrenic drug. Previously a healthy man, Plyushch became a physical wreck – and a mental one. Undoubtedly as a result of the international campaign mounted on his behalf and the efforts of his wife and friends inside the USSR, Plyushch and his family were granted exit visas and left the Soviet Union for the West in January 1976, as this book was going to press.

In this book, Plyushch's case is fully documented: from it we learn of the appalling sufferings which one man and his family have endured, and which many others like him, and their families, are enduring in the USSR at the present time. But this book contains as its centrepiece a collection of letters which Plyus'ch wrote to his wife, Tatyana, his two young

[c

continued from front flap]

Lesik, and his friends during a few months in 1973 from the special hospital before the effect of drugs made him incapable of writing any more. The letters are not about politics, but rather about his habitual concerns: the upbringing and intellectual and moral development of his sons, his own reading, games, and the everyday doings and welfare of his wife and everyone else dear to him. The man the KGB deemed too dangerous to be left at liberty will appear to the reader one of the most attractive and, above all, one of the most normal of men, a man in whom the 'two cultures', the liberal and the scientific, cohabited easily. As well as the letters, there is an essay, 'Moral Orientations' (1970), in which he deeply explores the moral implications of adherence to the democratic movement in the USSR – fascinating in its revelation of the wellsprings of that movement, and once again an indication of the quality of Plyushch's mind and the breadth of his culture. Plyushch's open letter, which led directly to his persecution, is also included.

This book was first put together in Moscow by Tatyana Khodorovich, a long-standing dissenter, and published in Russian by the Alexander Herzen Foundation in Amsterdam in 1974. The English edition has additional extracts from the *Chronicle of Current Events* to bring the record of Plyushch's case up to September 1975, and Plyushch's statement made after his release. Peter Reddaway, of the London School of Economics, contributes a new introduction.

THE CASE OF LEONID PLYUSHCH

Leonid Plyushch

The Case of Leonid Plyushch

Translated from the Russian by Marite Sapiets,
Peter Reddaway and Caryl Emerson

Editor of the Russian edition
Tatyana Khodorovich

Introduction by
Peter Reddaway

 C. Hurst & Company, London

First published in English by
C. Hurst & Co. (Publishers) Ltd.,
1–2 Henrietta Street, London WC2E 8PS, England

Russian edition *Istoriya bolezni Leonida Plyushcha*
© 1974, Alexander Herzen Foundation, Amsterdam

This edition:
Translation of Russian edition and of
Chronicle of Current Events, No. 36,
© 1976, C. Hurst & Co. (Publishers) Ltd.

Introduction © 1976 by Peter Reddaway
Chronicle of Current Events, all extracts except
No. 36, © 1974, 1975, Amnesty International

Translators:
Of essay 'Moral Orientations', Caryl Emerson
Of 'Open Letter to *Komsomolskaya Pravda*', Letter 1 and extracts from
Chronicle of Current Events, nos. 32, 34, 35 and 37, Peter Reddaway
Of all other material from Russian edition and of *Chronicle of Current
Events*, no. 36, Marite Sapiets

ISBN 0 903 983 50 8

Printed in Great Britain by
Billing & Sons Limited, Guildford, London and Worcester

CONTENTS

PLATES

INTRODUCTION TO THE ENGLISH EDITION
By Peter Reddaway

'There are people whose destiny it is to go far beyond the limits of their biography or background. They generalize many people's experiences and become symbols. The name of General Grigorenko has been such a symbol for five years. The same is true of the mathematician Leonid Plyushch.'

These words, written by the Soviet scholar Igor Shafarevich, are likely to echo and re-echo in the mind as the reader absorbs this book. For Leonid Plyushch has become a symbol of the resistance to a crime, and the pages that follow present poignant and irrefutable evidence of that crime.

The crime itself is probably as old as mankind, and doubtless it has occurred and recurred in various forms in all civilizations and cultures. Until recent times, though, it has not normally been regarded as criminal by its perpetrators: the individual dissenter has often been genuinely thought to be 'touched' or mad, and has therefore been isolated from society, sometimes to be 're-educated' This happened without society or its rulers thinking that anything wrong had been done. But with our enormous commitment since the Renaissance to the pursuit of knowledge, and with our deeper understanding of the human psyche, we have come, in the more advanced countries, to tolerate and understand dissent, and even – with pluralist politics, disestablished churches and secular universities – to institutionalize it.

In this context, the old tendency to regard the deviant as necessarily mad has gradually become insupportable. Thus when families, communities or states suddenly revert to it, opposition is now likely to appear. Indeed, sophisticated societies have devised elaborate mechanisms and procedures to try to *ensure* that it does, and that intolerance does not prevail.

In Russia, however, where the Renaissance was kept at arm's length until the eighteenth century, and where Western and Eastern traditions intermingle uneasily, no efficient mechanisms or procedures have been devised. Under the tsars, despite isolated incidents like the famous

Chaadayev case in 1836, there was no serious problem. But since the 1930s, when a political and ideological system aspiring to total control of the population was developed, the problem has become acute.

Under Stalin, paradoxically, the internment of real or imagined opponents in mental hospitals was often a much lesser evil than the alternative, which was probable death in a concentration camp. The hospital conditions seem usually to have been mild by comparison with those in the camps.

Only when the Great Terror ended with Stalin's death in 1953 did the situation gradually change. Now the population began to lose its atomized character, total fear receded, something resembling 'society' emerged, and along with it dissent and even opposition. As a result, Khrushchev was caught in a dilemma. He wished to rule by persuasion, not terror, yet the regime's ideology could not admit the existence of opposition. His solution was to exploit what, since the late Stalin years, had become the official and all-powerful school in Soviet psychiatry, that of Professor A. V. Snezhnevsky. This, among other things, effectively equated deviance with mental illness. Thus Khrushchev could have his cake and eat it: no terror and concentration camps, and also no dissent. Just a few madmen. . . .

But it was only in the second half of the 1960s, after he had fallen, that dissent became organized in the Soviet Union, and began to present a real problem to the regime. Now the punitive, deterrent and propagandistic functions of the expanding network of prison mental hospitals came to be exercised increasingly. More urgently than before, dissenters' ideas had to be discredited as those of madmen, because the ideas were starting to spread, both at home and abroad. And a more severe regime had to be introduced, including the forcible injection of powerful drugs, the aim being both to intimidate or even brainwash the dissenters into 'recanting' (and thus committing moral suicide and losing authority) and also to '*décourager les autres*'.

Hence the many documented cases of the last decade – like those of General Grigorenko and Victor Fainberg – recorded in the *Chronicle of Current Events* and other *samizdat* publications. Hence the term 'the da Vinci syndrome', coined in 1970 after psychiatrists examining the biologist Zhores Medvedev had fastened on his interest in politics as well as biology as a symptom of mental illness. And hence the semi-public lecture given in Moscow in 1973 by the psychiatrist Daniil Lunts, in which he described three people who were all suffering from different stages of a certain form of the progressive disease of schizophrenia: a person who criticized the Soviet social and political order; a person who hated policemen on principle; and a person who tried to assassinate high authorities. The task of the psychiatrist, Professor Lunts said, was to recognize this form of schizophrenia as soon as possible, at the first stage, and to try by treatment to prevent its otherwise inevitable progression to the second and third stages.

A number of features distinguish Soviet abuses of psychiatry from the sort of abuses which occur in most societies. The latter mostly involve attempts by families or small communities to suppress social deviance, or schemes by individuals to prevent relatives receiving inheritances, and other such sordid enterprises. Only rarely is it the trial prosecutor who insists that the accused is mentally ill when his relatives and the defence insist he is healthy. Much more often the reverse occurs.

In the Soviet Union, by contrast, the friends and relatives of the dissenters invariably (in the well-documented cases available) insist that the accused is mentally healthy, while only the prosecution and the official psychiatrists maintain the opposite. The initiative, in other words, derives from a state policy against dissenters, not from local complaints, prejudices or passions.

Secondly, the state has deliberately devised the legal and psychiatric procedures in such a way that its wishes will infallibly prevail. The defence has no right to choose even one psychiatrist for the original diagnostic team, nor for a team to give a second opinion, nor to call witnesses at the court hearing. It can ask for these things, but, enjoying no rights, it almost invariably has them refused out-of-hand.

Thirdly, there are no independent courts or other bodies to whom to appeal against a first court's decision. All courts, and the Procuracy, are under the regime's control, and so appeals are rejected.

And fourthly, there is no hope of redressing injustices by getting publicity in the press. All the media, too, are under the regime's control, and no dissenter has ever managed to have any protest or petition or article or letter to the editor published. Moreover, elaborate police measures operate to try to prevent such documents from circulating even in *samizdat*, i.e. in typescript copies passed from hand to hand.

In short, everything is done to preserve silence and secrecy. The system is essentially arbitrary, with only a veneer of apparent legality and of legal procedures. At the same time, however, it is also immensely bureaucratic, and this fact can somewhat reduce the arbitrariness. It also offers the dissenters and their friends some opportunities.

These points are well illustrated in this book,* which largely speaks for itself, mainly through the mouths of Leonid Plyushch and Tatyana Khodorovich.

Mrs. Khodorovich is a long-standing Moscow dissenter. In 1971 she was dismissed from the Academy of Science's Institute for the Russian Language after eighteen years of often praised work there as a researcher on Russian dialects and methods of teaching Russian in secondary schools. At the time of her dismissal the Institute's director said that her views were 'incompatible with the calling of a research officer in an institute of the Academy'. In recent years she has been prevented by the secret police from obtaining any employment. But despite continuing KGB harassment, she has persisted in a wide range of humanitarian activities. In May 1974 she and two colleagues openly handed to foreign correspondents in Moscow issues 28–30 of the *Chronicle of Current Events*, which had, prior to that, been successfully suppressed by the KGB for a year and a half.

Readers will be able to judge Plyushch's intellect and personality for themselves by reading his essay and letters and the testimony of his friends. They will note the breadth and depth of his interests, and his knowledge not only of Russian culture but also of the literature of the Ukraine, in whose capital, Kiev, he has spent most of his life. They will doubtless agree that he is not an activist by temperament, but rather a man of reflection and scholarship, with a driving intellectual curiosity about human behaviour and ethics.

Probably it is the integrity and 'wholeness' of his personality, rather than any exhibitionism or masochism, which require that he act out his ethical beliefs without fear. This would explain why he sacrificed his promising career in cybernetics in 1968 at the age of twenty-nine when, during the first broadly based confrontation between the regime and the dissenters, he spoke out in the open letter printed on pp. 3–6, denouncing the new wave of political trials. Doubtless, too, it was ethical commitment rather than any innate activism which caused him a year later to become a founder-member of the Moscow-based Initiative Group for the Defence of Human Rights in the USSR. This

---

* The legal points are examined by Mrs. Khodorovich in great detail, in relation to Plyushch's case, in a long analysis included in the Russian edition of this book, *Istoriya bolezni Leonida Plyushcha* (Alexander Herzen Foundation, Amsterdam, 1974), as additional appendix 2a. That edition contains a number of documents which have been omitted from this book to avoid unnecessary repetition, but which are of interest to the scholar.

was the first group of its kind, unsanctioned by the regime, to exist in the Soviet Union for over forty years. To belong as the only member in distant Kiev required special courage, and the KGB soon initiated serious attempts to frighten him into inactivity. Having had him sacked from his research job at the Academy of Sciences' Institute of Cybernetics the year before, it now raided his apartment, interrogated him, and arrested and tried some of his friends. Undeterred, he continued to sign the Initiative Group's appeals about the suppression of others. But in January 1972 he himself fell victim at last to a wave of arrests that swept the Ukraine.

What was the KGB to do with him? He had no history of any mental illness, but on the other hand he had not broken the law in any clear-cut way and he could not be intimidated into recantation. Moreover, he would speak out strongly in his own defence at a trial, and his friends would come from Moscow and elsewhere to demonstrate outside the courtroom. No, it would be simpler to have him ruled non-accountable by complaisant psychiatrists, and then he would not even be present at the hearing, which would be a brief formality. And this, with a number of technical complications, all described in this book,* was what in fact occurred.

The campaign to help Plyushch began among his friends in the Initiative Group, who included Tatyana Khodorovich, and was strongly supported by his wife, Tatyana Zhitnikova (who uses her maiden name). These people have kept up their unrelenting efforts for nearly four years now, enlisting eminent figures like Dr. Andrei Sakharov and sending a steady stream of appeals not just to Soviet bodies but also to psychiatrists, lawyers, mathematicians and humanitarians in the West.

The mathematicians have so far been the only group to make a strong and sustained response. In early 1974 they unified their efforts for two colleagues interned in mental hospitals by forming the 'International Committee of Mathematicians in Defence of Leonid Plyushch and Yury Shikhanovich'. This committee was based in France,† but quickly

---

* A full text of the final psychiatric diagnosis is given in Professor John Wing's forthcoming book, *Aspects of Schizophrenia* (London, 1976), but it is a Soviet translation and cannot be checked against the full Russian original, which is not available in the West. Professor Wing was given it in the Serbsky Institute, Moscow, in October 1973.

† Its secretary is Dr. Michel Broué, 18 rue du Gén. Pajol, 77130 Montereau, France.

developed support in other countries, notably in the USA, Canada, Britain, Germany, Italy, Holland, Australia, and Israel. Its regular bulletin has recorded numerous appeals and interventions for the two men, and also, in mid-1974, the release of Dr. Shikhanovich after an unprecedently short imprisonment. It also organized, in Paris in October 1975, what was probably the largest mass meeting in defence of a Soviet political prisoner ever staged, some 5,000 people attending.

Other groups especially active in Plyushch's defence have been the humanitarian organization Amnesty International and the London-based Working Group on the Internment of Dissenters in Mental Hospitals. And in 1975 the psychiatric profession began to stir from its apathy, the Royal College of Psychiatrists in London sending a strong protest to the Soviet authorities about their treatment of Plyushch and two other dissenters, treatment 'which appears a perversion of psychiatric practice and denial of natural justice'.

However inadequate the western response, Professor Shafarevich was probably accurate when he said in his statement quoted above, written for International Plyushch Day in April 1975: 'All of you who are concerned with Plyushch's fate are united not by parties, class, or national interest, but solely by the desire to save a human life, mentally and physically. The range and impetus of your endeavour is a ray of hope in our bitter age. But you are defending much more than just one person. You are defending all those who are in the same plight, whom the same misfortune has befallen, but whose names remain unknown to you.'

Plyushch's suffering is recorded in many of the pages which follow. So, in a few, is that of his wife and family. But perhaps the most vivid description of the latter has been given by a family friend, Victor Nekrasov, the well-known Kiev writer who was forced into emigration in 1974: 'I was always amazed: what self-discipline, what calmness and unshakability, what a capacity not to reveal how tough things are, what will-power and determination there was in this short, always smiling, whether sadly, ironically or scornfully, but always smiling woman. There were happy smiles too, even laughter, and very infectious, especially when she described the unthinkably stupid and primitive methods resorted to by the people whose job it was to break her will. Tanya had lots of humour – perhaps to some extent that is what saves her. Without it she could hardly carry on.'*

* See *The Observer*'s Colour Magazine, London, 20 July 1975.

A year later another family friend, Arkady Levin, an engineer, emigrated to Israel and brought a grimmer account: 'Plyushch's wife told me that Leonid speaks with difficulty, that either his jaw has been damaged or his vocal chords are partially paralysed. I think that Plyushch's wife is concealing his true condition, not only from her children and friends, but also from herself, so as not to yield to despair.'

And indeed, at the time of writing in October 1975, Plyushch's plight seems more desperate than ever. The Soviet authorities appear to be bent on using his case for broader, symbolic and very sinister purposes. As a key part of a more repressive policy against dissent in general, they have apparently opted for maximum brutality against Plyushch, precisely because he has a better organized lobby in his defence than any other single dissenter. Their aims seemingly are: first, to make Western humanitarian opinion give up and 'throw in the towel', out of a feeling that it has proved powerless to help Plyushch; secondly, to make it give up even more completely as regards other persecuted dissenters, on the grounds that the less well-organized lobbies in their defence could never succeed where the Plyushch lobby had failed; and thirdly, to intimidate other dissenters even more severely than hitherto, by proving to them that the KGB is now prepared not only to destroy them as human beings if the circumstances are convenient, but also to do so even if they might have a lobby like Plyushch's.

The grounds for accepting this interpretation are that while the campaign for Plyushch has grown steadily in strength over the last year and a half, the authorities have treated him with a continuing brutality, which, as time passes, has become ever more potentially fatal to his reason, and even to his life.

So far, Western humanitarian opinion has remained steadfast in the terrible trial of strength, rightly judging that, eventually, the Soviet authorities will probably give in when the pressure rises above a certain point. But, of course, no one can guarantee that an awful accident or tragedy will not occur before that point is reached.

October 1975

The hope expressed in the last paragraph above has, happily, come true. Plyushch was released on 9 January 1976, on the Hungarian-Soviet border, and put on a train to Vienna with his family. The pressure produced by the Paris meeting in October 1975 had been great enough to force the French Communist Party to jump on the band wagon, for fear of losing electoral support. It appealed publicly to the Kremlin to have Plyushch released, and in November the Soviet authorities decided that the game was no longer worth the candle.

On his arrival, Plyushch was pronounced by psychiatrists to show no signs of mental illness, just physical symptoms of profound exhaustion and of treatment with drugs harmful to his health. He indicated to the press that when he had fully recovered from these, in France, he wished to campaign for the sixty political inmates who remained in the Dnepropetrovsk Prison-Hospital, for his psychiatrist friend Dr. Semyon Gluzman, and for other victims of the KGB. He impressed all who met him with his modesty, intelligence, humour and kindness.*

12 January 1976   P.B.R.

* For Plyushch's first public statement in the West, see page 143.

INTRODUCTION TO THE RUSSIAN EDITION

By Tatyana Khodorovich

Leonid Plyushch was born in 1939 at Naryn, in the Tyan-Shan region of the Kirghiz Republic in Central Asia, into a civil servant's family. His father disappeared in 1941, and was never seen again. His mother worked as a cleaner. In 1956 Plyushch graduated from middle school with a silver medal, although he had been bedridden for four years with bone tuberculosis.

In 1962 he graduated from the Mechanical–Mathematical Faculty of Kiev University. In September of that year, he began to work as an engineer-mathematician in the Cybernetics Institute of the Ukrainian SSR Academy of Sciences. He worked on the modelling of biological systems and published the following articles: 'Mathematical Models for a System of Regulating the Level of Blood Sugar, using an analogue computer' (Seminar on 'Mathematical Models in Biology', 1965); 'An Evaluation of the Organization of Neuron Structures' (Scientific-Technical Conference on the occasion of Radio Day, 1966); and 'The Function of Proximity and Criteria of Self-organization' (in the collection *Bionics: Biosystem Modelling*, Kiev, 1966).

In 1968 Plyushch wrote a letter to the newspaper *Komsomolskaya Pravda** in answer to an article in that paper on the trial of A. Ginzburg and Y. Galanskov. In analysing the article, he showed the unsubstantiated nature of the charges, and referred to the trial itself as a regression to the judicial lynching methods of 1937.

In July 1968, Plyuschch was dismissed from the Cybernetics Institute in defiance of the Ukrainian SSR's laws on labour. Not long before his dismissal, he was given the following official reference:

Leonid Ivanovich Plyushch has been working as an engineer in Department 42 of the Cybernetics Institute of the Ukrainian SSR Academy of Sciences since 1962. During this time he has shown himself to be a thoughtful, hard-working employee; he has a creative, conscientious attitude to his work. Recently

---

* The official newspaper of the Communist Youth Organization. For the Text of this letter see Part I, pp. 3–5. *Tr.*

Plyushch has been taking an active part in work on themes involving psychology and engineering.

We must also point out the valuable social work which L. I. Plyushch has carried out in the Department, as a Komsomol organizer, and as a leader in the philosophy seminar devoted to practical problems of Marxist-Leninist ethics and aesthetics.

Head of Department
Y. G. Antamonov

Attempts to find a new job were unsuccessful: after his application form had been examined, he was always refused work.

Eventually, in May 1969, he obtained temporary work as a book-binder, but after he signed a letter sent to the UN by the Initiative Group for the Defence of Human Rights in the USSR, he was dismissed from this job as well.

On 15 January 1972, Plyushch was given his preliminary diagnosis 'Anti-Soviet agitation and propaganda', and arrested.

About a year and a half after his arrest, Plyushch was given permission to correspond, and letters began to be received from him.

I also received a letter. This letter, which bore witness to the originality and unusual nature of the author's mind, gave me the idea of collecting all the letters Plyushch had written from the Dnepropetrovsk psychiatric hospital, and publishing them. In order to do this, I asked his wife and his friends if they would allow me to read their letters from him.

I feel that these letters will convince any unprejudiced person (including non-psychiatrists) that Leonid Ivanovich Plyushch is not only mentally healthy, but has lost none of his former outstanding intellectual abilities.

Of the published letters, only No. 1 was written soon after his arrest, in January 1972; the rest were written in August and September 1973. They express a touching concern for his wife, his children and his friends, and a strong interest in anything related to the question of how and why we live. He devotes much space in his letters to his aim of continuing his interrupted work on philosophy and game psychology. In this connection he is interested in new books on structural analysis (the methods of which he uses in his studies of game morphology), on mythology (to check out theories on the origin and history of games) and on the mathematical theory of games (to check his own hypotheses when inventing experimental games). He describes new games he has created, also new stories for his sons,* made up behind the walls of his psychiatric prison.

Leonid Ivanovich's many interests are not chaotic, or random, or aimed at achieving an encyclopaedic, ivory-tower knowledge; they are purposeful, well thought-out and carefully chosen. His main interest is the theory of games, which has now become firmly established as a practical aid in modern scientific thinking. If the processes of professional scientific thought, so natural and necessary with science at its present level, have become a proof of mental disorder, then things are indeed terrible.

While reading Plyushch's letters, I began also to feel a terrible suspicion: has an attack begun on the 'precious inner world of man'? How else can one explain the fact that Plyushch is locked up among the insane?

---

* Three letters to Plyushch from his eight-year-old son have been included (see No. 17); clearly these are not without interest, as they reveal the boy's lively reaction to his father's letters.

PART ONE

LETTERS

OPEN LETTER TO THE EDITORS
OF *KOMSOMOLSKAYA PRAVDA*

I have before me the issue of your newspaper dated 28 February 1968 and a letter from Alexander Ginzburg's mother protesting against the libellous (as she describes it) article in the same newspaper of 18 January 1968. Yet again there is the contrast between the 'snivelling prevarications' (as Marx put it) of the censored press and the uncensored voice of *samizdat*. The point is – whom are we to believe? It is difficult to make a direct check – who is going to permit access to the records of the court hearing of the Ginzburg–Galanskov case? The only thing left is an indirect verification. I shall try to explain to you why I give no credence to the official version in this particular case.

Argument 1

For a very long time now our press has commanded no confidence whatever. High-pitched, screaming articles about 'enemies of the people', and then, [twenty years] later, little articles about 'the innocent sufferings of the heroes of the revolution and the civil war'; all the hubbub about the flourishing development of the countryside and then, later, a shamefaced mention of the millions of peasants who perished during the *artificial* famine of the 1930s in the Ukraine (that, at any rate, was the view taken of those events by Admiral Fedor Raskolnikov, Hero of the Revolution and the Civil War);* descriptions of 'Gestapo agent' Tito, and later the almost unnoticeable apology to the Yugoslav Communist Party;† the persecution of Pasternak which led to his premature death; the crazy 'Devil's Sabbath' performed during the routine crusade against culture in 1963; the glorification of 'our dear' N. S. Khrushchev, the current time-serving leader, and then the micro-

---

* In a letter to Stalin of 1939. *Tr.*

† In 1955. *Tr.*

doses of barbed hints and little stabbings directed at the 'voluntarist', ignorant boor, etc.;* the falsehoods about 'the anti-semite' Sinyavsky, alleged to be a hater even of Chekhov (I have read his 'Graphomaniacs' and been convinced *at first hand* of the falsity of the calumnies heaped upon the author); and the odious concoction in the periodical *Perets* aimed at one of the best Ukrainian critics, Ivan Dzyuba. Our press even presents true ideas in such unworthy form that one begins to have doubts about them too (e.g. the 'one-sided polemic' with Steinbeck).

In contrast to this torrent there is *samizdat.*

Are there any grounds for trusting the letter by Ginzburg's mother, the 'Appeal to World Public Opinion' by L. Bogoraz and P. Litvinov, the 'Appeal to Public Figures in Science, Culture and the Arts' of Gabai, Kim and Yakir? (Yakir is the son of the famous army commander who was martyred in Stalin's torture-chambers and slandered by the same press discussed above.)

In my view, there are.

Or are they, too, 'insufficiently well-informed' and 'misinformed by bourgeois propaganda'? Or in the pay of the NTS, the CIA, the BBC or the Voice of America? I hope you have not sunk to such absurdities.

If they were lying, then the KGB and its affiliated organizations would take pleasure in bringing libel actions against them – and they would not even have to pass special laws like the deplorable article 190 of the Russian Criminal Code. And anyway courage cannot be bought.

Argument 2

If the trial of Ginzburg and his friends had been lawful, there would have been no fear of making it an open one. True, Ovcharenko states that there were in court 'representatives of enterprises and organizations with which the defendants had been connected at various times'. But Litvinov and Yakir maintain that they were stooges. And I believe them, not Ovcharenko, since I saw with my own eyes a similar trial of so-called 'Ukrainian nationalists' in 1965 and listened to the fantastically stupid explana-

* After his fall in 1964. Tr.

tions by court officials regarding the 'open-closed' nature of the trial.

If the trial had been lawfully conducted, then *Komsomolskaya Pravda* would have published the letter of Ginzburg's mother and publicly, with facts – facts admitted by the same Yakir or Litvinov (even *Komsomolskaya Pravda* would not suspect them of denying facts in the form of search records and trial records as described by L. I. Ginzburg) – that would have proved the untruthfulness of her letter.

But – alas! – the times have passed when Bolsheviks proudly proclaimed: 'We don't fear the truth, as the truth works for us!' Their indirect heirs (the direct ones were destroyed in Stalin's torture chambers by Beria), the Thermidoreans of October [1917], fear truth. The most they can rise to is stereotyped and distorted quotations, thrown together at random.

After all, only with the truth would it have been possible to convince both our public opinion and the world's that the trial was lawful and just. For the times have passed when the naïve [German writer Leon] Feuchtwanger could persuade himself – at the trial of Radek, Pyatakov, Sokolnikov and the others – to believe in the comedy (till the end of his life he could not forgive himself for this).

Argument 3

The mendacity of the article is apparent even to the unaccustomed eye, unguided by past experience. The paper alleges that Ginzburg and Galanskov were 'paid NTS agents', and that they maintained 'strict conspiratorial secrecy' as befits agents of an anti-Soviet organization. And the same paper, in the very same article, writes that their 'concoctions' appeared abroad *under their own names*. But what about the conspiracy? Is all this conceivable? They ought at least to have learned how to lie in forty years of Thermidor!

Ovcharenko could not bring himself to name – among those who had 'swallowed the bait' of bourgeois propaganda – the people who signed the 'telegram of the fifteen' to Litvinov and Bogoraz-Daniel: Bertrand Russell (the conscience of Europe since the death of Romain Rolland), Igor Stravinsky, [J. B.] Priestley and the others. But he did not fear to distort Yu. Galanskov's final speech – his words about his lack of any desire for glory.

... I think there is only one point where Ovcharenko speaks the truth: 'Their names mean absolutely nothing to the Soviet reader.' Yes, just as the name [of the writer Mikhail] Bulgakov meant nothing to young readers a few years ago, and as the name of Ivanov-Razumnik* and many other names mean nothing to them to this very day. I pity those readers who do not know that there is a great Russian writer living and working in the land of Russia, Solzhenitsyn, the author of the novels *Cancer Ward* and *The First Circle*, and the plays *Candle in the Wind* and *The Tenderfoot and the Tramp*. I pity all the people who signed the letters published in *Komsomolskaya Pravda* on 28 February this year. They just didn't understand anything. Perhaps they will be shamed later, as those who marched in their thousands and 'angrily' demanded death for Lenin's comrades-in-arms are ashamed today. For they are not all in the ranks of the Black Hundreds; rather, they are descendants of the old woman who added her faggot to the bonfire of Jan Hus.† May God grant that they be cured of this 'saintly simplicity'. Then there will be no bonfires. . . .

I pity those who do not know, and do not wish to know, what has happened and is happening in their own land. In his letter to Stalin, [Admiral] Raskolnikov wrote that the people would judge him for all he had done with our revolution. I hope that that time will come, and that both Stalin and his lackeys will be judged in accordance with the laws of our country, and not in disregard of them. Thus, too, as distorters of truth, will you, the Editors of *Komsomolskaya Pravda*, be judged in accordance with the laws of honour. Under those laws you have already merited the contempt of all honest men, as lackeys and false-witnesses of our time.

L. I. Plyushch, mathematician and engineer
Kiev, March 1968

* The populist R. V. Ivanov-Razumnik.
† The medieval Czech martyr.

LETTERS TO HIS FAMILY AND FRIENDS

1. *To his Wife, Tatyana Zhitnikova*

My darling, dearest Tanchik!

Yesterday I received a parcel from you and it was almost as though I met you. Even your signature delighted me.

The only thing is that you've gone to too much trouble and not always with the right results. Oranges aren't any good, they seem somehow out of place, and I never eat onions (in general it seems that I'm not going to change most of my habits, except perhaps smoking, but even that not yet). The same goes for underclothes. It's not worth sending cheap stuff – after all, parcels aren't allowed very often. But enough about such trifles.

I feel quite normal, both physically and spiritually. And if it weren't for my thoughts about all of you, then with my five-year experience in a sanatorium none of this would alter my usual routine so very much. I have enough to eat. Books are available. I've got Shevchenko's *Tales*, Kvitko-Osnovyanenko's book, Dubov's *Boy beside the Sea*, a two-volume edition of Conrad, and Kochetov's *The Zhurbins*. I'm devouring Shevchenko, though of course his tales don't compare at all with his other works. One simply enjoys the inner integrity and refinement of soul that Repnina wrote about. You read and you see the world through his sad, passionate eyes. In his tales he is softer and more sentimental. Maybe, later, I'll really study 'The Bard'* and examine different aspects of his psycho-poetics (this term I've invented myself, and I'm not sure if I'll be able to explain it to you – something along the lines of: what it is in the Bard which reaches the heart, and how).

All these days I've been working on a game. For the moment not systematically, just pursuing parts of it, certain themes. Sometimes successfully, sometimes not. I feel drawn more to the psychology of the game than the morphology: the game centres, the exposition and working out (not philosophically, but psychologically – the exposition of the rules, the features, etc.), the stages,

---

* I.e. Shevchenko. *Tr.*

the system of the stages, etc. When it's finished they've promised to let you have it.

I'm hoping to work, as much as is possible with purely abstract thinking about games (though I'll be able to have a chess set), on: (*a*) functions in games, (*b*) components of games, (*c*) structures of games (in terms of their subject, material, processes, development), (*d*) transformations of games (at least a few), (*e*) the synthesis and putting-together of games (certain principles), (*f*) the effectiveness of the didactic aim and the construction of games, (*g*) the relevance of the subject to the various aspects of games. If I'm feeling up to it I'll try to construct several experimental games which are suitable for experiments and also good just as games. I'd specially like to work at nardy.* They contain so many possibilities. If you can, hand in some cubes for me (although I'll be able to use some makeshifts, e.g. the pages of books – but that'll be clumsy).

If you'd like, I can write down in my next letters the basic elements of what I manage to do.

How are things for you at work? How are your lectures and your practical work? Are they understanding you?†

I'm very glad that I managed to read Vygotsky on pre-school education. If you can, send me some quotations from that article, everything you think important, plus what he puts in italics. I've just written down everything I remember, but of course that doesn't give me his precise definitions. And he makes them very incisive. If you have time, do the same with his whole book – the italics or the main formulations (not the polemical ones, but first and foremost the positive ones). The same with any structuralist articles, if you can get hold of good ones. The same with Elkonin. But all this is only if you have the time and inclination to read them. Yes! As regards Elkonin, only what he writes on infancy and the pre-school period (without the physiology), and on the nursery-school period whatever you choose.

---

* A dice game.

† Plyushch's wife worked, until she was dismissed as a form of harassment, in the department for pre-school education of the Ukrainian Ministry of Education.

Tatyana Zhitnikova, the wife of Leonid Plyushch, with Viktor Nekrasov, 1974.

Mama should evidently be informed. But she and Ada* should not get alarmed and travel here in a rush. As regards a meeting with me (if Mama does come), judge the situation yourself – I wouldn't want to frustrate her completely.

Write lots about Dima†. Only the truth (about yourself and Lesik too, about everything) – if not, I'll be making all sorts of suppositions.

Dima! My son who's almost grown up! You write something to me as well, at least a few lines (providing they're not formal). As regards helping Mama, and your school work, I won't say anything. I think you'll take care of those things by yourself. Describe to me some interesting adventures or books (museums, journeys – you know how much I like all those things).

And now Lesik too! It's a pity I didn't have a chance to say

* Plyushch's sister.
† His elder son; the younger son is Lesik. *Tr.*

good-bye to you – you were asleep and were seeing something nice in your dream. Well, what should I describe for you? If you like, in each letter I'll send you a 'bedtime story', so that Dima and Mama can read it to you. Then there will be 'Papa's story time', when the 'bedtime stories' are read. And if I can't think up a story I'll try riddles or puzzles. And if I can't think them up either, then I'll try some games – for Dima and you (if Dima wants). But which do you prefer (stories, riddles, or games) and about what? Put in your order.

It's a pity that I wont' be able now to write a short story for Dima – it won't work. If you were keen on maths, then I could try to think up some sort of puzzles with fairy-tale or humorous themes, as in Bobrov's 'Magic Bull'.

Tanchik! If anything is unclear about 'Cats–Mice', 'The Invisible Woman', 'Dynamo' or 'Trinards',* write and I'll try to write the rules better.

Darling one, my dream . . .†

Greetings to all our relatives and friends.

Your Robinson, Shiva and all that.

20.1.72

2. *To T. S. Khodorovich*

Dear Tatyana Sergeyevna!

I was overjoyed to receive your letter. But I must confess to you quite openly that I don't like writing letters, and I don't know how to, owing to a peculiar epistolary complex. I am usually dry and awkward in letters. So that, with regard to what you wrote about your own awkwardness of expression, there is nothing to choose between us. I was very pleased by what you said about Lesik. If you did not write your impression of Dima because you didn't want to offend me, it was quite unnecessary. He interests me more at the moment because he is at a decisive age. Tanya‡ will have told you, no doubt, that all my arguments with her concerned

---

* Games invented by Plyushch.

† Some words here were deleted by the prison censor.

‡ His wife. *Tr.*

'honesty towards oneself' (a phrase used by Vinnichenko* in the novel of the same title). I feel that both social and individual psychological problems come down to the problem of man's conscious control over himself (and over society, i.e. over himself as a species). But to achieve this, we must learn to look at ourselves clear-sightedly – both as individuals and as a species. From this standpoint I am critical of Tolstoy and of every religious-ethical point of view. Tolstoy could not tolerate the truth about himself, about people near and far from himself, and he compiled a myth, which helped him to hide away from reality. Even Nietzsche behaved in the same way. On the plane of personality, this led to their both becoming the playthings of their own subconscious. This is clear from the nature of Nietzsche's sickness, which revealed that behind his anti-Christian battle against God lay a search for God, for Christ. I feel that, to be his own master, man must first become aware of his own unconscious motives and wishes. It is for this reason that the environment into which the personality has been 'thrown' should be seen quite clearly. Otherwise the personality will become the plaything of surrounding factors. Freud's mistake (one of his mistakes) was that he ignored the part played by the external environment. Fromm and other neo-Freudians are trying to rectify psychoanalysis by making it more socially orientated, but all I know of their work is what others have told me.

Let us regard the preceding lines as a gauntlet thrown down in challenge to you and Tanya, as Tolstoy's supporters. Unfortunately, I don't know you at all well, and so perhaps I am merely initiating a discussion to no purpose (maybe you are opposed to argument, as an unproductive form of dialogue?). In our circumstances, the possibilities for a discussion between us are very limited, and maybe this also makes it undesirable. I just want to make my position on Tolstoy clear. I am very enthusiastic about his criticism of all facets of civilization. There is only one pretentious aspect of this criticism – over-simplification of his

* *V. K. Vinnichenko*, Ukrainian novelist (1880–1951), who emigrated in the 1920s. Described in the Large Soviet Encyclopaedia as a 'bourgeois nationalist'. *Tr.*

The editor, Tatyana Khodorovich, 1974. Left, Sergei Kovalyov (see page 105).

opponent's position. (Tanya has perhaps told you about my line concerning Tolstoy's criticism of the Trinity, a 'common-sense' line which affects to disbelieve the existence of dialectical logic, and of a higher mathematics, in which, for infinite numbers, one may be equal to three. It is in exactly the same way that Tolstoy over-simplifies the materialist standpoint.) In this respect Dostoyevsky is deeper and therefore more honest and true to himself (except in *The Devils*, where the Nechayev's figure is over-condensed and over-simplified).

On the positive side, I only like some aspects in him – his concept of 'corruption' in art, his theory about 'temptation', parts of his educational theory and ethics. What I like is not his system as a whole but some parts of it.

I would be very glad if you could tell me something of what is new in the field of structural analysis. Unfortunately, I have read little about analysis. For instance, on this subject I have read a little on intellectual game analysis, but this was superficial and even terminologically inaccurate. Structural analysis interests me mainly from the point of view of structural interpretation. For example, Propp's* historical interpretation of the fairy tale interests me more than the structure of the fairy tale. What interests me even more is a psychological interpretation of fairy tale structure, which complements that of Propp. Without such an interpretation modern pedagogical theories about fairy tales will not, it seems, be able to say anything substantial.

In the past year and a half I have been studying the structure and psychology of witticisms (and comedy in general), analysing 'Kobzar',† and studying especially the psychology of intellectual and physical games. I have substantially increased my under-standing of games, especially through the analysis of emotional balance in them.

I have not had any particularly interesting results from my study of Shevchenko. I think this is because my approach to his work is not the right one.

I have only just started an analysis of humour. Luk has a good system of classification in his book on the emotions. My own notes differ somewhat from his conclusions. But even here I am more interested in the psychological interpretation of structure than in structure itself. When the structure has been revealed, one can then take a step beyond Freud in analysing wit.

I should like to analyse traditional folk riddles and proverbs from this standpoint. The riddles first began to interest me largely because it seemed that the guessing of the solution was not their primary purpose (children are not interested in solving folk riddles, nor are they able to do so. But riddles set by teachers have a recognizable educational function, as children are able to solve them. This should be checked through experiments). Folklore riddles – like folk proverbs – have an aesthetic, metaphorical function (I disregard here their differences, their specific individual

* *Vladimir Yakovlevich Propp* (1895–1970, a philologist and folklore expert, author of *The Morphology of the Fairy Story* and *The Origins of the Fairy Story*. Tr.

† A long poem by the nineteenth-century Ukrainian poet *Taras Shevchenko*. Tr.

elements). In 'Frost-Red-Nose', Nekrasov,* I feel, very often uses riddles as constant images.

It's a great pity that linguistics doesn't interest me at all. However, I am trying to read articles on structural linguistics, in order fully to understand the structuralist method.

(By the way, let me make use of the fact that you are a linguist: how much of a connection is there between the pairs of words 'humour' and '*mort*' (death) and '*amour*' and '*mort*'? A link exists in Russian and other languages. Is the only connection in the Russian word '*umorit*'?† If there is a deeper connection, I was thinking of linking this with an analysis of the word 'comic'.)

It's interesting that both you and I have been reading Shchedrin‡ at the same time (this is in answer to your mention of him).

Well, now I've told you approximately what has been of interest to me recently. Tanya writes that you have been studying the question of ethics in scholarly activity. This interests me as well – because of the influence of Tolstoy, whom I really got bound up in some ten years ago.

My mood at the moment is uncreative and non-epistolary – I can't for the moment dissociate myself from my surroundings. That makes my letter all the more dry, but I feel you will make appropriate allowances for me.

Give my greetings to all my friends, especially Nina Nekipelova, Grisha and Masha, and everyone, everyone.

Write if you feel like it. I shall answer you, also depending on my mood – so that we shan't bore each other.

Your

Lyonya§

---

* *Nikolai Nekrasov* (1821–77), poet, who popularized folklore. *Tr.*

† The Russian word *umorit* can mean either 'to kill' or, alternatively, 'to reduce someone to uncontrollable laughter'. *Tr.*

‡ *Saltykov-Shchedrin*, a nineteenth-century Russian realist writer. *Tr.*

§ Lyonya is an affectionate form of Leonid. *Tr.*

3. *To his Wife*

Hallo, darling!

Hallo there, Dima and Lesik!

It's a great pity that your visit didn't come off. The photographs are a poor substitute although, of course, I'm very happy to have them at last.

Judging from the photographs, you haven't taken up gymnastics after all. Pity.

I have nothing worth while to write about myself at the moment. I'm in good spirits. The book situation here is very bad, and so I'm pinning great hopes on you. It will not be possible for me to receive many books, and we'll have to think over carefully what exactly you could buy for me. Of all the books you sent me, the most valuable for me was the book on structuralism. Janson's fairy story was likeable, but, even disregarding the awful translation, it's not a necessity. The same applies to Lifshits and Gardner* (I admit I haven't read them yet and I may change my mind about them).

I need books on structuralism, on the psychology of emotion, pre-school psychology, serious works on games (all kinds – from manipulative games to intellectual ones), works on the psychology of mythological thought, on fairy tales, etc.

What I need most at the moment are the works of Vygotsky (in full), Elkonin's *Child Psychology*, a photocopy or your own account of Leontyev's article on games (1946?), Markov's book, and Gurvich's article (on time) in *Questions of Philosophy*.† Works on the psychology of emotion are the most important. It would be good to write to Luk and ask him for his book on emotions and a list of books and articles on this theme. I have unexpectedly found some evidence to support P. Solomonov's 'informational theory' of emotions, so I should like to re-read his work. Linkova mentioned some monograph by Davydov on emotions.

* Not clear from context which authors are referred to. *Tr.*

† *L. S. Vygotsky*, a Soviet psychologist of the 1920s and 1930s. Founded his own school of psychology. *A. N. Leontyev* and *D. B. Elkonin*, psychologists of the Vygotsky school. *A. A. Markov*, a Soviet mathematician. *G. D. Gurvich* (1894–1965), sociologist and positivist, who emigrated in 1921 and published many works abroad on social structure. *Tr.*

I have written a draft article 'The Construction of the Intellectual Game', and so I've now transferred my interest to the question of emotional balance in a game. Maybe I'll manage to write an article for *Knowledge is Strength** about *nardy* and *gusky*.†
But for that I'll need Gurvich, Propp, Bakhtin, Losev‡ and Batishchev are of secondary importance (no, Bakhtin is really necessary, especially his article on the activity of man's essence – borrow that from Arkady. It would be good to write to Batishchev, asking him to say which of his works are concerned with pedagogical theory (and letting him know our own conclusions, in summarized form).

Now for the order-list. First of all, I'd like *Questions of Philosophy*, *Questions of Literature* and *Questions of Psychology* (if they have not deteriorated lately).§ Secondly, I'd like the *Literary Gazette* and *Science and Life*.

Now let us turn to parcels. I need sugar and butter. Buy the cheaper tobacco, in larger quantities. In any case, don't go out of your way over parcels. On your next visit, bring a pair of hospital pyjamas, just in case. And buy a toothbrush and some toothpowder.

I'll stop now. I don't feel in the mood for writing. I probably won't be able to continue my work on the humorous element in games. But I will be thinking about these problems and so I'll need books.

I'm not writing to mother for the moment – could you write to her?

I'm waiting for your visit.

4. *To his Wife*

My dear sunshine!

I am continuing my reply to your four letters.

* Popular science magazine, published in Moscow *Tr.*
† Dice games. *Tr.*
‡ *M. M. Bakhtin*, a Soviet literary critic; author of a book *Dostoevsky* (1929) and a work on the comic-grotesque quality of Rabelais. *A. F. Losev*, Soviet philologist and philosopher, author of numerous works on myth and symbolism. *Tr.*
§ Soviet monthly journals. *Tr.*

I'm still at the stage of getting myself adapted to my surroundings. If I were to try to express, in a short formula, the position I have chosen to adopt, it would be the motto of the three wise monkeys (remember, the ivory ones): 'hear no evil, see no evil, speak no evil'. However paradoxical it may be, it seems to me that the best form of psychical self-defence here is a special kind of 'conscious autism'. This will be difficult for me, because of my extrovert character and my tendency to be outward-going.

The books and letters I get from you, and my reflections on games theory and related questions connected, these will have to be my supports.

This is all I can say about myself.

Your letters are wonderful and true. I shall answer them in order, beginning with the first.

Ada, you and Tatyana Sergeyevna all join in praising Lesik. Write to me in more detail about both of them. I was on the point of compiling a list of books for them, which it would be worth reading to them. I'll have to write it down.

I have also written out a list of summer 'hobbies' for Lesik: observing nature, and 'experiments' with natural objects. This will add some real substance to his interest in nature.

In my letters from Kiev* I tried to explain my point of view on the purposeful influencing of child development. A first-rate example of this is the way 'scribbles' can be developed into drawing. At first, a child draws meaningless scribbles. But it is easy enough for an adult to explain to him that 'scribbles' can have a meaning, and the process of scribbling begins to acquire a level of meaning, and this is followed by a change for the better on the purely technical level in the customary drawing. The development of each facet of character, each ability, is made more effective in precisely the same way – by raising the level of meaning, by enriching them, by imbuing them with new meaning.

If Lesik applies himself consciously to his observation of nature, then this will obviously develop his powers of observation, his

---

* These letters were never received.

interest and his understanding of the logic of the natural sciences more effectively than spontaneous observation would.

Even if you do not receive my letters, I shall try to go into greater detail about the 'scribbles' (in a generalized sense). This is an essential addition to the generalization of emotions and explains to some extent the concept of sublimation.

By the way, could you get hold of Stendhal's article on love (Vol. 4 of *Collected Works*). In it he introduces the concept of crystallization of feeling. Have there not been any scientific investigations of this concept?

I was very pleased to read what you said about Dima's thoughts and his essays on literature and biology (on evolution). Write to me about him in even more detail than you do about Lesik, as I have absolutely no idea what interests him at the moment. I should like to resume my correspondence with him in a way which he would find interesting. I don't think there would be much point in Lesik writing to me. He wouldn't be interested in writing letters. If I'm wrong about this, I should be very glad.

What do you read to him? You write that his bedside book is *Lives of the Animals*. I doubt if he reads it much. But he could try to read some of the stories by Bianchi and Prishvin.*

I've already written to you from Kiev about Dima's reading. I think the basis of his reading matter should be romantic in character: the romance of conflict, scientific search, travel, friendship, love and so on. You know what worries me about him – so write about him in greater detail.

You write that you will be going out to work from 30 August onwards. Surely you mean 30 July?

I've already written about parcels and books. I don't think there should be any point in your sending me all the issues you've already received of *Questions of Literature*, *Questions of Philosophy* and *Vsesvit*.† Pick out whatever is especially interesting.

Besides the explanations of intellectual games, I've received

---

* *V. V. Bianchi*, 1920s Soviet writer of children's stories, mostly about nature. *M. M. Prishvin*, Soviet writer (1873–1954), author of numerous stories, mostly about nature. *Tr.*

† Ukrainian paper. *Tr.*

more detailed descriptions, and a clear analysis, of outdoor games, in particular of how to classify them. I should also like to have some material on construction games and games involving the manipulation of objects.

You write that nothing much has changed in the world around you. And then you go on to give an abundance of news. I'm very happy for Sasha and Tamara. I think they'll be happy. I congratulate them on their son. How big he is already! I embrace their whole vast household. By the way, you misunderstood – in your second letter you speak of 'children' and not of their child. From this phrase I concluded either that you visited them together with Lesik, or that there was some other child there. Did I guess right, I wonder? (As you see, I have not abandoned Freud, although I approach him warily.)

I'm very glad, although a little surprised, about your growing friendship with Maia. I often remember her, and our arguments. I hope – tell her this while giving her my greetings – that she will be of help to me in my polemics against Tolstoy.

Who was it who 'grew small and disappeared'?

How is Larissa? I'm very sorry that our last conversation remained unfinished and that she misunderstood what I meant. If she is still in Kiev, then explain to her that I reproached her precisely because, in contrast to my feelings towards Boris, I respect and honour her as a person. I care less than nothing about Khlestakov.* Anyway, you remember what it was I got cross with her about. One is always more severe with someone one respects – that's so obvious that it's banal.

Give my greetings to Ira and her daughters. How is Sergei's Ira adapting to her new role? I won't object if she wants to write to me herself (even if it's only by adding a few lines to your letter).

You haven't written anything about Zampira.† And I've been troubled all this time because I couldn't reply to her. I wrote to her from Kiev, but I wasn't allowed to send the letter, though I

---

* Chief character in Gogol's *Inspector-General*. Exact meaning here unclear: perhaps a derogatory nick-name for Boris. *Tr.*

† *Zampira Asanova*, a Crimean Tatar doctor, and leader of the Tatar national movement. *Tr.*

explained to them how necessary it was. I'm worried in case she may be annoyed with me. What kind of mood is she in at the moment?

I've already asked about Klara. What you told me about Slava* came as a complete surprise for me. My warmest greetings to him. You say he's 'full of creative plans'. What kind of plans? You know my attitude towards his literary efforts. I feel that he will produce something worth while only if he adopts a more realistic standpoint; in my view, 'modernist' elements merely spoil his stories. Ask Viktor Platonovich and Galina Viktorovna† what they think. I would be glad to get a letter from them, but please don't mention that to them.

Write to me in more detail about Sharapov's letters. We were only together for six to eight days, but we became extraordinarily friendly. I'm still amazed about this. How is he? Couldn't we help him in some way? He really wanted to 'get in touch' again, and it would be a pity if a camp were to swallow him up again without trace. He's one of my pleasantest memories in this past year and a half. Has the other Viktor, from Moscow, been writing to you? Find out about him from G. I haven't the same feeling of spiritual affinity with him, but I would be very interested to hear what has been happening to him. He ought to have been released some time last year. If he writes, ask him what has happened to our third neighbour, Felix Lifshits.

I should really like to start corresponding with N. V. and E. L. but evidently they don't have a chance to write. Give them my warmest greetings and say I'm longing to meet them again.

Let me go on to the fourth letter. You write about Herzen,‡ about your impressions of his correspondence with Natalie. It's strange how closely your views tallied with my own reaction to

* Slava – *Semyon Gluzman*, a psychiatrist, sentenced to ten years in labour camp and exile under Article 62 of the Ukrainian Criminal Code, in October 1972.

† *Viktor Platonovich Nekrasov* – writer, author of 'In the Trenches of Stalingrad' (living in the West since autumn 1974). *Galina Viktorovna* – V. P. Nekrasov's wife. *Tr.*

‡ Nineteenth-century Russian writer; *My Life and Thoughts* is his autobiography. *Tr.*

the corresponding chapters in *My Life and Thoughts*. Their letters produced a strongly sympathetic response in me too – a feeling that they were in some way familiar and close to me (emotionally speaking). It is not clear to me what the 'various notes written after going abroad' are about. If this refers to the unsavoury pathological episode with Herweg,* then I can say that it made a depressing impression on me as well.

Don't bother to send me Herzen – in accordance with the principle I've already referred to, of keeping to material that is absolutely necessary and interesting.

Let me return to you. I feel (judging by all the circumstances) that this business will last a long time. (I want to continue the conversation we began on that last evening.) And if that is so, you must arrange your life independently of me to some extent. It would be the greatest mistake on our part if you were to concentrate your life just on writing to me, sending me parcels and thinking about me. There's no point in turning a real life into one based on illusions or part-illusions. I for one will also try to break the pattern, to broaden my emotional life beyond the limits of my correspondence with you.

You know my attitude to asceticism. To constrict one's life, in whatever way, is a worse sin than most (perhaps only shackling someone else's is worse). I should not like to feel that your thoughts of me were inhibiting your life in any way. I love you, my dream, more than anything else in the world, more than creation itself, and I would not want to become your inner chain.

I shall not refer to this matter in future, so don't reply to these words of mine. If you think about it seriously, you will agree with me that there is nothing worse than to feel that someone you love is tied to you by chains. For the same reason I wouldn't like you to represent me to the children as some kind of noble hero, on the lines of the Cid, as an example to be constantly looked up to.

Similarly, I don't want anyone to write to me out of 'a sense of duty', and I don't want you to hide unpleasant things from me. I prefer to look reality in the face and make my decisions con-

---

* Probably a nickname. *Tr.*

sciously. This is the same old 'honesty towards oneself' that Vinnichenko advocates.

I'll stop now. Give my greetings to everyone. If you visit Leonida Pavlovna (?), greet Ivan Alekseyevich and Nadiika* especially. It's a pity that he and I never got round to studying structural analysis together.

Good-bye for now, my dear. I haven't written to Mother. I'm waiting for her letter.

5. *To his Wife*

I'll try to reconstruct, from memory, the rules of the transformation game I invented for Dima's birthday. Unfortunately, I haven't been able to try the game out with anyone. So you'll have to test all four variants yourself.

Variant No. 1. Use a chess-board (8 × 8). The players have sixty pieces each (differentiated by colour or in some other way). The pieces are cubes, with the sides numbered from 1 to 6 (or with some other signs differentiating the cube surfaces). The players take turns to place the pieces on the board, one by one, with the number 1 facing upwards. If a piece on the board forms a 'quadrant' with three other figures, a transformation of the pieces takes place. Examples of quadrants:

	1	2	3	4	5	6	
F				I			
E							
D		3		2		I	(1) A1, A2, B1, B2
C	2		2				(2) B2, C1, C3, D2
B	I	I		I			(3) B2, B4, D2, D4
A	I	I					(4) B4, D2, D6, F4

Transformation takes place in the following way:

In quadrant No. 1, all the figures are removed, but one of them changes its surface number to '2'. In the second quadrant B2

---

* Probably I. A. Svitlychny and his sister Nadiya Svitlychna, Ukrainian dissenters who had in fact been arrested in 1972. *Tr.*

changes its surface number to '2'. Later all pieces with the number '2' on them are removed, and replaced by one piece with the number '3' facing upwards (there are two transformations here: B2 changes from '1' to '2', and then '2' changes to '3'. But as D2 already has '3' on it, it is not removed. There are two transformations because, after the first transformation, quadrants remain in the same squares).

In the third quadrant, one of the two pieces, either B2 or B4, is removed while the other changes its number to '2' (i.e. the piece is turned over).

In the fourth quadrant, three pieces are removed, leaving one piece with the surface number '2'. If the square B2 had remained empty, and all the others were as shown on the diagram, then three quadrants would be transformed; they would be completed by a piece numbered '1' being placed on the square B2. The end result depends on the order of transformation.

First variation of play: First, in quadrant No. 2, change the surface number of B2 from '1' to '2'; then, in quadrant No. 1, remove all the pieces with '1' facing upwards (three altogether), and change, for example, the piece on square A1 to read '2'. After this, in quadrant No. 3, on square B4 change the surface number to '2', and then remove all the pieces with '2' on them, replacing them on square B2, by the number '3' (or 'troika' as I say for short). The remaining quadrant, No. 3, contains two 'troikas' and two 'twos'. We remove the 'twos' and put a 'troika' on square C1. The board as a whole looks like this after sequence of play:

	1	2	3	4	5	6
F				1		
E						
D		3				1
C	3					
B		3				
A	2					

Second variation of play: Put a '1' on square B2. Remove all the

pieces in quadrant No. 1 and replace them by a 'two' on square
A1. The sequence of play ends thus:

	1	2	3	4	5	6
F						
E						
D		3		2		1
C	2		2			
B				1		
A	1					

　　In the first variation, transformation is compulsory. If a player
has not changed his numbers on completing the squares (not
noticing or not wishing to), his opponent can remove any piece
bearing the smallest number (for instance, in quadrant No. 4, he
can remove any piece with '1' on it, but he must put a piece of his
own in its place. In the other variations of play this does not occur.
　　In the second variation, if a player does not change numbers at
the right time, he is not allowed to change them later.
　　A piece reading '2' counts as 1 point; a piece with '3' on it as
5 points, '4' as 25 points, '5' as 125 points, '6' as 625 points. The
purpose of the game is to obtain the maximum number of points.
In the fourth variation, it is to gain the piece with the highest
number (four, five, six).
　　The game ends when all the squares are occupied. In the fourth
variation, it ends when one player gets a '6', or when no further
play is possible.
　　In the third and fourth variations, the players can transform not
only newly formed quadrants but also old ones. (No more than
three quadrants can be transformed in one move.) Unfortunately,
I can't remember all the rules, and it's not possible for me to
reconstruct the game by playing it with myself.
　　The game has turned out to be very interesting, somehow.
Instead of a hierarchy of numbers, you can use a hierarchy of
subjects (mouse – hare – fox – wolf – tiger – lion). It should be
realised that the game is complicated, and for older schoolboys

(perhaps even middle-school age) appropriate subjects should be found. However, choose the artistic design for the game yourself (not only the shape of the pieces, but the names of the game, the pieces, the moves, the quadrants, etc.).

When you've tried out the game, write me your impressions of it. It could be made very intreesting.

I'll send the game for Lesik next time – the didactic one for learning multiplication.

I may have forgotten some of the rules of the game – I'll fill those in later. Have you managed to make out the rules I've written down?

I would really like you to be able to do some work on my games.

The transformation game is especially important to me. For it is the type of game envisaged by theory.* I 'sought' it for a long time, and it is, for the time being, the only example of a whole species (actually, it is the fourth variation which is the real transformation game).

You write that you've bought the two-volume edition of Hegel. What does it contain? If it has the 'Phenomenology of the Spirit' in it, send it in the next parcel.

I've looked through Nos. 5, 8 and 12 of *Science and Life*. I've re-written '*Alkuerk*' and '*Chisolo*'.† Nothing new in the way of theories. In No. 8 there was an interesting article on pleasures. Send it to me.

---

* *The following note has been provided by Dr Roman Rutman, a Moscow scientist and dissenter who emigrated from the Soviet Union in 1972 and is now a professor in the department of electrical engineering, Toronto University:*

Games theory is a branch of mathematics in which the 'game' is seen as a formal mathematical model of a conflict situation: a player acts against an opponent whose moves in reply he cannot know in advance. Games theory involves studying this uncertain situation and choosing the best strategy, i.e. the best actions for the player.

Games theory creates a mathematical basis for a cybernetics approach to games. Another component of the cybernetics approach is the psychology of games. A cybernetic analysis of conflict situations is useful in solving certain problems in economics, sociology and military affairs. (*Translated by Peter Reddaway.*)

† The names of games, both here exactly transliterated. *Tr.*

6. *To his Wife*

My darling!

I have just discovered that you have not yet received even one of my letters. And that this is only because I write about subjects outside the limits of 'ordinary life'.

I find it hard to confine myself to expressing myself like an idiot: I'm alive, and in good health, I eat well, I sleep too, I hope you too are 'well' – but I'll try to do it in this letter.

My condition – physically – is normal, anyway. I can hardly wait for your visit. I received a parcel from Mother. Consult with her about visits, gifts and parcels. Don't send perishable goods. It would be better if everything was sent off by you, but Mother won't agree to that. I'd like to have more frequent visits from you, but for that you'll have to coordinate the visits among yourselves.

I've received seven books. I've already written to you that my main interest is in books on games and their psychology, on educational theory, on structural analysis. The book on traditions in Kiev was very interesting, and the others had two or three good articles each.

Soon, it seems, they intend to start giving me haloperidol (or galoperidol), a Hungarian drug. What this is exactly, you can easily find out. I have already observed its effects. Brrr. . . .

I've received Dima's letter. A very good one. No letters from Ada or from Mother.

What you write about Lesik continues to please me greatly. In the spring, I worked out a nature-study plan for him. It's too bad that it will almost all be out of date by now; and they won't give me back the plan, with all my papers.

Write and tell me what the possibilities are for getting my games officially accepted for production.

Both the games I sent you seemed quite interesting to me, especially the one meant for Dima. After all, this is a new sort. . . .*

It would seem that I shall have to give up smoking. We are allowed three cigarettes a day; occasionally we get more.

This is all I can say about 'ordinary life' here. I should have

---

* Rest of sentence blacked out by the censor.

liked to give my opinion about the books you sent, and to begin an account of the results obtained in Kiev. But it can't be helped.

Tanya, write to me regardless of whether my letters are frequent or not. You see what can easily happen.

Goodbye for now.

P.S. I doubt whether you did the right thing concerning Lesik. But you know the circumstances better, of course.

Try and get hold of my letters to you, and the ones I wrote to Mother, Dima and Lesik (one each), which I handed in for posting before my transfer here. I was promised that they would be sent. There are no reasonable grounds for withholding the letters.

7. *To his Wife*

My dear one,

It's three days now since you left. I've received your letter. You wrote about Z. Pelegri's *Horses in Town*. In future, write in the same way about films and books. There's no need to send me literary works, I think – it's more important for me to receive scientific literature. Although I'm beginning to have my doubts about the use of scientific literature. . . .* For this reason I shall go on writing to the children. I've had letters from Tamara and Sasha, from Julia Alexandrovna and V. Nedobora.† I don't know if I'll be able to answer them. Explain the situation to them, in any case. I'm very grateful for their letters. But I won't always be able to answer them.‡

Your news about M.'s collapse is very sad – although it was already in its early stages when I was still around. And no one can really help him – everything depends on himself.

Don't send every copy of *Questions of Philosophy* and other journals; just pick out the interesting issues and send them. I don't think *Knowledge is Strength* is likely to be of great interest.

* A gap follows, where the censor has blacked out a section.

† *Vladislav Nedobora*, a friend of Plyushch from Kharkov, sentenced to three years' forced labour (1970–3) for his human rights activity. *Tr.*

‡ In addition to being forced to live among mentally sick people, and to the frequent impossibility of using a pen or paper freely under those conditions, Plyushch was now being subjected to 'treatment' with haloperidol.

№5

Здравствуй, родная!

Уже 3 дня как ты уехала. Я получил твоё шестое письмо. Ты пишешь о "Лошади в городе" Ж. Тел- гу. В будущем пиши так же — о фильмах и книгах. Художественное, видимо, высылать не нужно — более важно получать научную литературу. Хотя я начинаю сомневаться в целесообразности научной литературы — ~~...~~ По этой причине я не буду сегодня писать детям. Получил письма от Тамары и Саши, от Юлии Александровны, от В. Недобо- ра. Смогу ли ответить им — не знаю. Ты в любом случае объясни им ситуацию. За их письма очень благодарен, но отвечать не всегда смогу.

Рассказ об упадке Мирона очень грустен, хотя началось это ещё при мне. И помочь здесь действительно невозможно — всё зависит только от него самого.

"Вопросы философии" и другие журналы отбирай — только то присылай, что интересно. "Знание-Сила" вряд ли представляет большой интерес.

Занимается ли кто-нибудь ненормальными играми? Я думаю или забыл, кое-что сделал уже. Лишь изучив их в сово- купности можно будет раскрыть суть поведения игры, суть игрового воспитания, развития.

Original of Letter 7, written from the 'special psychiatric hospital' at Dnepropetrovsk, showing deletions by the censor.

Is anyone studying the subject of non-intellectual games? I'd like to study this, and I've already done some work on it. Only by studying such games as a whole can one discover what the essential concept of a game is, what is its educational function, how it develops.

Tanya, send Mother this letter – or write to her yourself – I still haven't received their letters and I can't think of anything else to write to them; I've already sent one letter, and I am now waiting for the reply.

I kiss and embrace you all.

Lyonya

26.8.73

8. *To his Wife and Younger Son*

My dear, far away star!

I've received your seventh letter. I've also had letters from Ada and Viktor Sharapov. I hope Ada and Mother can come next week. I'm sending a letter for Viktor to you.

I feel a little better and I'm very sorry that I wasn't in good spirits during your visit. I've only just realised what it was you wanted from me. I'm reading the papers carefully.

Of course my point of view has always been based on ethics, not politics. I didn't understand your question about that.

I unfortunately still don't know which of my letters you have received. So I don't know whether to repeat what kind of books and parcels I need.

I'll repeat, very briefly, what sort of books I wanted. Everything on structural analysis (not the purely linguistic side, only what contains extrapolations). Secondly, Propp, Bakhtin, Vygotsky, Leontyev, Markov and Venger. In short, I need everything on structural and psychological analysis.

I'll ask a doctor if I can have Freud and Jung sent to me. I'm interested in those works by Freud which I haven't yet read: 'Introduction to Jensen's novel *Gradiva*', and his article on Leonardo da Vinci. *Wit and the Unconscious* would be too bulky to send.

You had better read these two articles. If you can't send photocopies of them, you could then at least tell me about their basic themes, and the methods of analysis used. Both articles are in the Academy of Sciences library. I intend to subscribe to the *Literary Gazette* from here. I'm waiting impatiently to read *Notes from Tartu University*.*

I don't have my notebook to hand. That's where I wrote down the books that interest me. For example, last year a new book by Lotman† came out, on structural literary criticism. Did you miss it? Now that you know some of the structuralists personally, ask them about new items. My main interests are structural myth-analysis, literary criticism, folklore and psychology (we don't yet have anything published on structural psychology here, I think). Is Lévi-Strauss going to be published?

Of the new books you handed in, only Meletinsky's‡ book *The Fairy-Tale Hero* was of real interest to me. It's a pity that it's out of date and too highly specialised. Besides that, I've read the *Italian Plays*. These are almost all splendid. I liked *The Heart of the Family* best. The ending seemed to me awkward, however – too much discussion, spoiling the artistic tapestry as a whole. All the philosophizing should be within the bounds of the artistic creation, not outside it. Also interesting is the anti-fascist play, the first one.

Have you read Meletinsky yourself? You should find the chapter on Ivan the Fool§ interesting. It's a pity that the author hasn't developed his own point of view; so Gorky's view, though one-sided, is better. I find his observations linking the image of Ivan the Fool with Prince Myshkin¶ very significant.

I would extend this link to Don Quixote and even to Christ, or more precisely, to Christ's paradoxical concept of the 'poor in heart' in the Gospels. 'Poor in heart' seems to have a double meaning. First, the 'poor in heart' are the seekers, 'hungering and thirsting' for the truth (I don't remember the exact phrase in the

* Periodical publication of this Estonian university. *Tr.*

† *Yury Lotman*, a Tartu University literary scholar. *Tr.*

‡ *Eleazar Moiseyevich Meletinsky* (born 1918), literary critic and folklorist. *Tr.*

§ A character in a Russian folk-tale. He is the third brother, the 'fool', who marries the princess in the end, and confounds his two 'clever' brothers. *Tr.*

¶ The hero of Dostoyevsky's novel *The Idiot*. *Tr.*

Gospels). Secondly, they are the democratic masses, in opposition to the 'scribes' and Sadducees, with their half-baked book-knowledge, dead and stagnant.

If you haven't read Meletinsky, then do so. His book contains some information on games and their links with ritual. Here are some quotations: 'Dolls played an important role in the life of various peoples. They were considered to contain the soul of a dead person, so the doll had to be fed' . . . 'The game of blind man's buff may originally have had a ritual meaning. It represented the trials of the huntsman at the hands of the bear, master of the forest.' Among his remarks on other books, I found even more detailed descriptions of the link between generic games and ritual, ceremonies and myths. For instance, lawn-tennis was a sacred fortune-telling game among the North American Indians. Evidently, special studies exist of the mythological and ritual sources of generic games. I should like to develop a similar hypothesis about 'nards', based on structural analysis, and by means of this, to show the meaning of the morphology of games.

Meletinsky is also interesting for his varied observations on the didactic nature of stories. We'll obviously have to study the psychological and educational aspects of fairy-stories, in connection with the child's period of development through games and stories (i.e. up to the age of 10–12 years). He makes an interesting observation – that in myths the cultured hero and creator is often accompanied by an inept or stupid brother. If, though, there is no brother, then he unites in himself the role of creator and of magician. This is very close to Miron's idea of the 'circus criterion' in children's literature, his concept of poetry as 'man can do all, the fool can do nothing', as an overcoming by the child of his inferioirity complex. Could you send me the relevant works by Miron? Also his book on Marshak,* on Marshak's 'anti-entropy'. Give him my greetings.

I can picture the changes you've made in the children's rooms, and of course I approve. I would have loved to take part in this, and in transforming our own room.

---

* *S. Y. Marshak* (1887–1964), Soviet poet, translator and literary critic. *Tr.*

Write and tell me how Lesik reacted to my 'début' as a story-writer. I only have one more episode planned. Write more about the children. And about yourself, darling.

2.9.73

Good morning, Lesik!

I've got your letter at long last. A pity it was so short.

I'll tell you what would be a good plan from now on: you write your letters over a number of days. Whenever something interesting happens, write it down in your letter to me. Write about any new books you've read.

I've written a lot of stories for you, about how 'Daddy was once a little boy', and 'Wonderful and terrible adventures of little Papa, little Aunt Ada and other little grown-ups'. But I can't send them to you just yet. With this letter I'm sending you a present for your birthday – a game. Let Dima and Mama show you how to play it. But this game is only for someone who knows how to multiply. If you don't yet know how to do so, I'll send you another game, and you'll be able to play this one later. Write and tell me what sort of games you like. Have you learnt to play '*ugolki*'* and '*diamino*' yet?

Did you like the new story about Moomintroll? I liked 'Moomintroll and the Comet' better. It was a happier story, and funnier. Don't you think so?

I'll make up some stories about the letter-eaters† later, after I've sent you the stories about the little grown-ups.

Mama tells me you've grown much braver and hardly ever cry nowadays. Good boy. Are you still afraid of the dark, as you were in the infants' school? If you are, then remember what I told you to do.

What have you been collecting on your walks this year? Do you collect plants, or only beetles?

I'd like you to carry out some experiments and observations on your own (or with Dima's help). It's a pity the summer is already

---

* Literally 'little corners'. *Tr.*

† Plyushch made up a 'Story about Letter-eaters' for his children on New Year's Day 1972 (he was arrested on 15 January 1972).

over, which means that some of them will have to be left until next year.

1. Lesik once caught some caterpillars and put each one of them into a closed box of its own. When he opened the boxes after two months, he found butterflies in them, but in one of the boxes he found a black wasp. He guessed how the butterflies came to be there, but was very puzzled by the wasp. I don't know if Lesik understood this in the end, or not. If Lesik hasn't read about this, let him observe more often how caterpillars turn into larvae, and what happens to them next.

That is a difficult task, but here's an easier one.

2. Put a wet cloth, with a piece of dough on it, in an uncovered place where you can easily see it. You can do this with meat as well. After a few days, examine it, and put it in a closed tin. Keep the bit of cloth wet all the time. You will find that maggots begin to breed in the dough (or meat). Where do they come from? They couldn't have crept into the tin.

To check how this happens, keep observing the maggots in the tin, and see what happens to them.

You won't get this to happen in winter. Why? And now try putting the cloth with the dough straight into the closed tin. There won't be any maggots. Why?

Now are you beginning to guess what happened to the caterpillars in the first experiment?

I've thought up a lot of problems and experiments like these for you. If you find them interesting, I'll describe some others to you.

Mama writes that you'd like to get a hazel-brown dormouse. In *Science and Life* (1972) there was a story about striped squirrels. They're very interesting too, and you can buy them in Moscow.

And now I'll go on to the game. I'll describe it to Mama.

Goodbye, my little reed-mouse. (I'll try to write you a story about reed-mice – fairy-tale animals.)

Lesik's Game

The board for the game is flat; it can either be rectangular in shape, squared like a chequer-board, or round, with the squares forming concentric circles (or circles in a spiral). There can be either 36 or

100 small squares on it. The game is to be played by two persons. The counters are two-sided (as in Reversi*). There can be either 36 or 100 counters.

The two dice can either be the usual cubes, or the Chinese variety of dice (10-sided, numbered from 1 to 10).

Each player in turn throws the two dice together. The two numbers that turn up are multiplied one by the other. The player places a counter (with his own side upwards) on the square on which the number corresponds to that resulting from the multiplied dice number, or else he can make as many moves with a counter already on the board as the total given by the multiplication. If both possible squares are already occupied, he misses his turn.

The game ends when all the squares are occupied (or, perhaps, in order to speed up the game, when all the squares numbered higher than 5 are occupied. Whichever you prefer). After this comes about, each player adds up all the numbers on the squares taken by his counters. The player with the highest total is the winner. This procedure, and the additions involved, takes a long time and might prove boring. The game can be ended more quickly if (instead of each player adding up all the figures on his squares) the two players cancel out any numbers they both have, by adding together two, three or more square numbers. Another simplification is by cancelling out pairs that match, like this:

A	B			B	A

It is easy to see that, in such a case, the total of the counters on one side is equal to that of the other. These simplifications are objectified rules, methods of simplifying algebraic equations, and this increases the didactic value of the game. The basic didactic aim is the learning of the multiplication tables from 1 to 6 and from 1 to 10 (either variant can be played on the same board).

The game is one of strategy.

How is the design on the board to be drawn up? An artistic design, I think – colourful, graphic, formalized, abstract.

* Game on draughts-board with counters coloured differently above and below (*Concise Oxford Dictionary*). Tr.

The dice are called '*Le*' and '*Sik*'; the game is called '*Le-Sik*' (but let Lesik himself speak up – do you like that name, Lesik?).

By the way, the fact that it is not clear which die is '*Le*' and which is '*Sik*' is inherently linked with the law of permutation in multiplication.

Unfortunately, I don't have my old Kiev notes to hand, in which I analysed this game from a didactic point of view.

9. *To his Younger Son*

Dear Lesik,

I've made up a little story for you, but I can't send it just yet. Did you get the game I thought up for your birthday? Write and tell me if you liked it. Write all about your games and books. And now it's time for the fairy-tale I promised you. First I'll tell you what a reed-mouse is. This is my present to you to celebrate the start of your second year at school.

The Reed-Mouse Dimle

You'll be asking, who might Dimle be and how can he be a reed-mouse? You can easily guess, by reading the title of the story carefully.

Any first-year schoolboy will know at once that a reed-mouse is a very small mouse. Any second-year schoolboy will realize that it lives in a reed. But only a very perceptive second-year schoolboy would guess that our reed-mouse acquired his name, Dimle, with the help of two brothers – Dima and Lesik.

Our reed-mouse lives, not in a reed-bed, but actually inside a reed. For a reed, like its relative the bamboo, is a long tube, divided into storeys by partitions of light, soft material.

And up above, on top of the whole reed-house, is an unusual feathery roof, a brush-roof. In this roof other beings live – all kinds of beetles and midges.

When the reed-mouse first started living on the ground floor of the reed, he was not very pleased with it; his whole apartment consisted of one dark, damp room – after all, it was just above the surface of the water in the pond. When the wind blew quite gently on the roof of Dimle's house, the brush-roof tried to hide from it by bending down among the other reeds – and then the whole reed-house creaked grumpily, brushed against the other reed-houses and involuntarily bent so low that Dimle's ground-floor room was soon under water. (At this point, let Dima draw how this happened, and what the reed-mouse was doing. But first he should practise drawing the picture and consult you and Mama about how to draw it.)

But the reed-mouse's distress didn't last for long – he just gnawed a hole in the floor and crawled into the cellar. The cellar walls were wet and slimy, and slippery. And before he knew what was happening, he found himself in the water.

'Brrrr . . . it's freezing!' shouted the reed-mouse, and climbed back into his room. But his room was even more wet now than it had been before – water had seeped in through the hole in the floor.

Dimle decided to move up to the next storey. It was nice and dry there. When he saw there was no one else living on the first floor, he realized that he would have not only an apartment with many rooms but one with many storeys. Climbing upwards from one floor to the next, Dimle reached the roof. The beetles and midges, seeing the new resident, at first began to buzz from fright and ran around in confusion. But when a dragonfly, flying past the reed-dwelling, scornfully remarked 'It's only a reed-mouse, you know', they were ashamed of themselves and went back to what they had been doing. Everyone knew that reed-mice are the most good-natured rodents in the world. They eat only all sorts of grain, and drink the dew from the feathery tops and leaves of reeds (to make this sweeter, they add 'reed-sugar' – dried bits of sweet-sedge roots and roots of other swamp and pond plants). But most of all they love the delicate taste of nectar and pollen, like the bees do. When a reed-mouse climbs out of a flower it's difficult to recognize him: his little snout and body are completely covered from head to tail with yellow pollen. He climbs to the very top of a plant, and he then licks himself all over, beginning from the tail and ending with his nose. The hardest part of all is licking away the pollen from the hair between his eyes (any second-year schoolboy, however unenlightened, can discover for himself how difficult this is – even if he has a very long tongue).

And, somehow, the pollen on his eyebrows, and between them, seemed to Dimle the most tasty. He always left this to the last, as a kind of after-dinner sweet.

After such a tasty wash, reed-mice look as clean and fresh as if they had only just come out into the world.

If you ever have a reed-mouse living with you, and you want him to be clean, dirty him up regularly. Dirty reed-mice are the cleanest reed-mice in the world. Every well-read expert on reed-mice knows this for a fact.

But you must know what to dirty them with. If you smear a reed-mouse with dirt or ashes, he'll remain dirty. Don't ever try to smear him with salt or mustard – he would be very upset, and would never lick his little fingers again. He might even leave you – and how sad you would feel then.

However, with what joy, what satisfied smiles and ecstatic squeaks a reed-mouse washes himself when smeared with cherry jam, honey, clotted cream and cocoa, or milk jelly. All these smearing substances are like soap to the reed-mouse.

But let's return to the reed-mouse Dimle. He does not, as yet, even suspect the existence of pollen, let alone the other tasty things.

After warming himself up in the sunshine, Dimle went back into the reed-house and started to make his apartment comfortable. The first thing Dimle had to do was to make a simple rope-ladder from long reed leaves, along which he could run up and down, from the roof to the cellar and back again. After he had plunged a few more times into the 'bathroom' – as he had named the cellar – Dimle climbed back again on to the roof and sat down to dry himself. The air smelt sweetly of nectar and of pollen from the plants around him.

Dimle wanted to go straight off and have breakfast, but he felt there was something missing in his apartment. Reed-mice love light, and it was so dark in his apartment! After thinking about it for a while, he began to bite out windows in the walls. Bright rays of light flooded the rooms, and beams of sunshine began to dance on the walls.

Dimle started chasing them, but the sunbeams refused to be caught. Even when he jumped onto one, it immediately sprang away and sat on his back. (Lesik knows all about that – it was just when he had covered a sunbeam with his hand that it sneaked out, and sat on the back of his hand.)

Dimle was in full chase after the sunbeams when, suddenly, he heard music. It flowed in from the windows and from somewhere in the depths of the reed-house. The reeds swayed with the sound, which kept changing as their movements did. The amazed Dimle put his head out of a window. The music changed again. In his surprise, Dimle's tail stuck up, covering another window. The music changed yet again. Dimle turned his head from one side to the other, trying to see where the musicians were. But, apart from the usual, quite unmusical flies, beetles, dragon-flies and butterflies, there was no one to be seen. Then, suddenly, Dimle guessed what it was – for reed-mice are extremely intelligent mice. The musician was . . . But I shall tell you that next time.

And did Lesik guess? Write and ask me whatever you want to know about reed-mice. Let Dima send me his picture of the reed-mouse Dimle. Do you like drawing? Or singing, or listening to music?

Write to me about all that.

Papa

2.9.73

10. *To his Elder Son*

Dear Dima,

I was delighted to get your splendid already grown-up letter. I've had a number of letters from Mama, in which she wrote about you. It was mostly pleasant reading. I was especially pleased by what Mama and Aunt Ada said about your essays. It's a good thing that you don't write about rubbish, but about serious subjects. Do you remember our discussions on that point?

I sent you, from Kiev, a more detailed letter about the essays, so I won't repeat myself.

. I confess that your low marks at school don't worry me much yet, because Mama writes that you're beginning to develop your own independent interests and your own individual thoughts (such as your essay on evolution, your concept of 'thought-emotions'). I sent you a letter from Kiev on the subject of 'thought-emotions'; it's funny how I, too, got very interested in this question recently (and still am). I have just written you another letter as well, about sophistry, sophist theories and the Sophists themselves – in connection with your inclination to sophistical argument. But don't get worried: I haven't written a lecture, I just try to describe the positive and the negative features of the ancient Greek Sophists, and I try to explain the harm that a liking for sophistry can do to a contemporary person's thinking.

If this theme interests you, I'll send the letter.

I was very surprised to hear that you like algebra better than geometry. As you have leanings towards art and sculpture, I should have expected that geometry would interest you more. By the way, I too loved algebra the best.

So you've completely abandoned your drawing and modelling. That's a pity. But do continue your study of art – even if it is only as an onlooker.

Your mother and I didn't have the right kind of education during our childhood, and so when we grew up we suddenly realized that we were completely ignorant as far as art was concerned. Especially in regard to music. And this is a pity – we have lost so many happy moments. You have the opportunity to achieve a far higher standard of culture than we had (in art, for example). Write and tell me what you think about this.

Do you help Lesik with his lessons? I'm going to send him some 'tasks', to develop his natural scientific interests. Help him carefully – don't try to make up his mind for him, let him think for himself, but give him a nudge in the right direction without his noticing. Mama will help you. Play with him (but – so that you both have an equal chance – give way to him surreptitiously in games where you're much better than he is).

I don't know how long you'll be in Odessa, so I'm sending this reply to Kiev.

I'm expecting your mother in a day. I would have been glad to see you as well, but then you're still in Odessa.

Goodbye. Write more about yourself and about Lesik.

Papa

11. *To his Wife*

My dear ones,

My sunshine,

I'll begin by clearing up a few practical matters.

I'm allowed to order certain journals and newspapers from here. But as we had already agreed that you would order the *Library Gazette* for me, I haven't ordered it myself. Though you'll have to send the appropriate receipt to me here. Do that as soon as you have taken out the subscription. It seems we'll have to do the same with the journals. Could you get a copy of the receipt for yourself as well (just to be on the safe side)?

If you send me money, include some extra kopecks (e.g. 10 roubles + 15 kopecks). Experience has proved that the money arrives sooner if sent like that.

As regards parcels, besides the things we've already talked about, I need meat and cheese.

Well, that's all the practical business finished for the time being.

I'd like you to give me more details about your pending visits.

You said that Miron had not yet published his articles on Marshak and on his 'circus-criterion'. I think you are mistaken about this. Something on those lines has been published.

I'm waiting impatiently for Maia's letters. I'm afraid I won't be able to answer them on the same level. But I want to emphasize again that I don't want people to force themselves to write to me. Least of all Maia.

I'm really enjoying the Tartu *Works*. I should like to exchange impressions with you about what I've read so far.

Do you remember our discussion about Propp's attempt to solve the problem of the structure and origin of the fairy-tale, how he never touched upon the question of the fairy-tale's psychological and educational significance, its importance in the upbringing of children? According to the publishers, he has indeed, in his works over the past ten years, analysed folklore from three angles, including that of 'collective function'. Could you find out in which of his works he writes about this? Perhaps he can shed some light on the social, educational meaning of fairy-tales at the present time.

The article on the structural analysis of fairy-tales (by Meletinsky and others) is interesting because of the parallels it draws between fairy-tales and games. But I'll come to that later (the authors examine various aspects of the structure of the fairy-tale, which agree very closely with Vygotsky's conclusions and closely resemble the step-by-step structure of intellectual games).

Of the two articles I've read so far, I found the first, by Toporov, especially interesting, as it supports some of my own ideas about riddles (remember, I spoke to you about this?).

'The cottage full of people, that has no windows and no doors.'*

This riddle could never in fact be solved, not even by adults, let alone children, unless . . . they already knew the answer. An experiment on these lines could be carried out – a group of adults (as intellectual as can be) would be given a selection of riddles, folk-riddles. They wouldn't be able to solve most of them. But they could solve riddles made up by educationalists for children. Why? Surely because the social function of folk riddles is different from that of 'educational-cultural' ones.

Educational riddles are a specific variety, a kind of logical problem. Their social function is didactic, designed to teach and develop the intellect. The social function of the popular riddles of folklore is different. What is their function? This is what we must discover. I think that riddles have the same function as regularly-used labels or metaphors – primarily an artistic function. If they are meant to develop any faculty, then it must be the ability to conceive images.

This function of folk-riddles has been noted by Nekrasov, who uses it to great effect in 'Orina, the Soldier's Mother' (or is it in 'Frost-Red-Nose'? I forget exactly which one). That folk-riddles are not meant to be solved is proved by the various solutions that can apply to each one, by the vague way in which the riddle is phrased. The riddle seems to be a particular form of the proverb (the function of the proverb being, in the same way, not connected merely with common sense or with 'popular wisdom'; but that is a more complicated question).

* The answer to this riddle is 'a cucumber'. *Tr.*

Toporov writes of the ceremonial, the sacred-ritual origins of riddles. 'In essence, it is often taken for granted that the solution to the riddle cannot be found by the uninitiated.'

The riddle first originated as a kind of myth-recitation (question and answer) dialogue, the kind of memorized dialogue used for marriage rituals, New Year ceremonies, etc. Thus there was no actual detection of the solution to the riddle, because the answer was already known, having previously been learned as part of the ritual dialogue.

It follows that, in ancient times at any rate, riddles were not guessing-games, games which had to be solved. Toporov mentions some other facts, which back up my surmise.

Maija, what do you think?

15.9

16.9 – I've received your letters (numbers 13 to 18) and two from Dima. I'm answering all your letters in turn. I've replied to all letters from friends.

Everyone keeps writing and praising Lesik. I would be interested to hear about his shortcomings as well. I've already written to you that I'm afraid his interests are of a superficial, collection-and-hoarding character. You wrote how he, together with yourself and with the help of Peter Nikitich, had made a collection of stones. I'm glad that he has a more developed attitude for that type of study. But I fear that we may be repeating the same mistakes which we made over Dima – making his study-tasks too easy, encouraging a sense of dependence, linked with a superficial personal approach. After all, he did not collect those stones himself. Even if he collected some of them, it wasn't with school-studies in mind.

From your letter I've guessed (in a roundabout way) that Lesik attends the school in Bessarabka Street. Be more precise. I'm somewhat afraid of the influence of that place. You know what I mean.

Dima's letters are very good. But try (tactfully) to get him to write while his memory is still fresh about something he is interested in (whether this is some event or something he's read or thought about, for instance his ideas about 'thought-emotions'). Then I too could write in a more interesting way to him. But whatever he does, he is not to write letters to me as a kind of duty.

I was pleased, of course, by what you wrote about your achievements regarding the fulfilment in your life of the commandment 'do not be angry'. But Tolstoy has nothing to do with this, really (or rather, Tolstoyan philosophy hasn't). That is a rationalization of your own behaviour and self-control. I haven't anything against most of Tolstoy's personal views. I like many of his ideas. But I reject his religious substructure and his excessive rationalization, which led to simplification and insipidity of ideology.

I really regret that I won't be able to take part in your work on the importance of intellectual games in the mental development of pre-school-age children. I don't have my notes on this to hand.

Besides the theses of Vygotsky and Elkonin, please do make notes on the great significance of emotional fulfilment for productivity in any kind of work, and especially in intellectual logical activities. This is usually not appreciated. An exception to this is Sukhomlinsky.* Read his works again. It's a pity that I can't quote from Rolland's *Enchanted Soul* (about his son Marc's education with the aid of 'joy'. It also has some splendid passages on 'forced behaviour', on overcoming difficulties, also on extra 'enjoyment'), or from V. Kuznetsov's† *Einstein* (on Einstein's own statements about 'the associative game of the mind', intuition; Kuznetsov's comments on the emotions).

I should have collected a lot of quotable material over this past year and a half – through my thesis work on this subject. Do write about your theses – I'll remember something to write in reply.

Note that mental functions range from interpsychical activity to inner thought (in Vygotsky, from quarrels to monological, proof-motivated, reasoned thought). A game is a 'dialogue', an interpsychical activity. It is an original argument, in which children learn how to collect 'evidence' in order to solve their

---

* *Vasily Alekseyevich Sukhomlinsky* (born 1918), pedagogue and education expert. *Tr.*

† *V. D. Kuznetsov*, Soviet physicist and mathematician. *Tr.*

problems, step by step. The basic component of intellectual game structure is step–by–step construction. The game's task – intellectual and emotional – is broken down into a succession of steps, of mini-tasks. A child begins by formally breaking down the intellectual process into stages, under the influence of rules. Having learned to do this, he spontaneously, when solving puzzles, divides his activity into stages.

If this interests you, I could try to explain it in more detail.

It's very important to demonstrate that this is a twofold division – emotional and intellectual. The basic unit of game structure, the move, is both emotional and intellectual (in solving the mini-problem of each move). The emotional aspect of the move is as follows.

The *uncertainty* of the move (the uncertainty of waiting, clearly apparent in the pure chance situation, independent of the player, the uncertainty of choice – how, where, etc., to move) produces emotional tension. The solution of each move, each uncertainty leads to emotional release low.

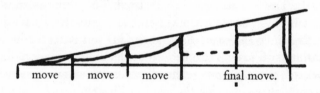

| move | move | move | final move. |

The general tension grows from move to move, until it ends in the final release. The structure of various games differs to some extent, but this is the general picture. Get the collection of essays *Topical Problems of Sexual Pathology* (pp. 68–71?). It contains Vasilchenko's article 'Structural analysis of apparent impotence' (I think that was the title), and it also contains a structural scheme of frictional (move by move) build-up of the 'sexual process'.

The scheme is amazingly similar to the one I've produced. This seemingly shows the unity of structure in emotional processes.

On the other hand, this process is very close to the emotional process of reading a literary work (the elements of division into moves, growth of tension, partial release, final release) – Vygotsky discusses this in his *Psychology of Art*.

I shall end there, on the subject of my work. I'll wait for your reactions.

Don't send me Kagan's* book – it's only for specialists. I suspect it won't be to my taste or connected with my subject. *Early Forms of Art* seems interesting and is obviously connected with games, fairy-tales and myths.

Don't bother to send me Stendhal – read him yourself. He describes the process of 'crystallization' of the emotions, inwardly connected with the process of 'taming'. Sukhomlinsky, too, mentions the links between 'taming' and the subject-role game of the emotions. I wrote you a letter about this link. But try to perceive it for yourself, through reading Prishvin's† stories 'Root of Life' and 'Drop of Water', Saint-Exupéry's 'Little Prince', the *Forsyte Saga* (following the theme of seizure, of appropriation, as opposed to 'taming').‡

What you write about Miron is very sad. The worst of it is that no one can help him. In the end, everything depends on his own efforts. He can only get out of the position he is in by 'rational' means. Otherwise he'll be broken by circumstances.

The passages you quoted on games and education were very interesting. It would seem that, in spite of everything, we've surpassed the Americans in the theoretical field. I was also cheered by the fact that my concept that 'everyone is, by nature, talented' is being confirmed.

I don't need the extract on the trial. The extracts on games will be of interest, but you must reproduce the corresponding games (so that we can build up a collection of games).

I agree with you that our centre of gravity must be in our own selves. But if it is only in our selves, it will never be enough. 'A unity in itself is a nought', and so on. There should be some relationship between the individual and the species (our centre of gravity is not in individual persons, or even in groups, but in the

---

* *V. F. Kagan*, Soviet mathematician. *Tr.*

† *Mikhail Prishvin* (1873–1954), writer and ethnographer. *Tr.*

‡ Russian *priruchenie*, meaning achievement of an intimate relation with a non-human object, e.g. nature, animals. Cannot be directly rendered in English. *Tr.*

human race as a whole, in its potential for good, which is created in particular by the good in persons which have created an individual centre of gravity 'within' themselves).

So now I've answered all your wonderful letters. Wonderful, because they satisfy my longings.

My greetings to all our friends.

Your Lyonya, my little star

Don't send your letters by airmail – I won't receive them any faster.

12. *To his Elder Son*

Dear Dima,

I've received two of your letters and two of the extracts you cut out from journals.

I liked the extracts very much – both of them, but specially the one about dolphins. You say that you can't think of anything to write about. Well, you could have written about those articles. What did you think about all that? That's exactly what interests me – what you're working on, what you like, what you've been reading and thinking about.

For example, Mama wrote me an interesting letter about your concept of 'thought–emotions'. I myself would find it interesting to have a letter from you on this subject. I, too, have often thought about this question, and I have some ideas on the deep links between emotions and thoughts. Perhaps your ideas are quite different from mine – if so, it would be all the more interesting to exchange views.

I am sceptical about Dadashev. Ask Mama to tell you how we verified what Messing* said; Messing had views similar to those of Dadashev.† He describes his experiences even more wonderfully, but when we tried to verify his statements there was no proof of anything except ideo–generic movement.

---

* Wulf Messing, famous hypnotist and psychic expert; a Jew, said to have escaped from a Nazi concentration camp by hypnotizing the guards. Emigrated to the Soviet Union. *Tr.*

† Possibly *Khizgiya Dadashev* (1860–1945), folklorist. *Tr.*

I don't exclude the possibility that Dadashev is more interesting than Messing, but I doubt it.

In my opinion, all wonders ought to be looked upon with caution – they should be carefully verified, even if they may seem impressive. Otherwise science is superseded by religion's belief in the miraculous.

That is the reason why I found the article on dolphins more interesting – it was written by scientists, not journalists. Scientists are usually careful when stating their conclusions.

My opinion on the article? I'm not an expert in that field. But I should be glad if it were proved that dolphins are capable of intelligent thought and have some kind of culture of their own. I was especially astonished by the fact that over 10,000 dolphins (of the Indian Ocean variety) had gathered together in one place. How could this be explained without recourse to hypotheses about intelligent thought?

I was surprised by your saying that you are interested in technology. I really never expected that! And, to tell the truth, I even doubt it somewhat. Be precise – do you like reading about technological achievements, or about the actual construction of technology, new technological working principles, etc.?

In the first instance, you can't really say that you're interested in technology. You are merely interested in its achievements (a little like football fans being interested in football – not as the footballers themselves are interested in it).

What games do you like to play? Who are your friends? Write about your friends, the people in your class. Try to understand that I want to know more about you, just as I want to know more about Lesik. Write to me about Lesik.

What would you like me to write to you about? Are you interested in *Knowledge is Power*? Some good artists are working for that paper. Or have you completely lost interest in art?

Well, goodbye for now. Write when you feel you want to do so.

Papa

Lesik! You write to me as well.

It's a pity that I can't go on with my story for you at the moment. Write and tell me how you liked the beginning. Perhaps you'd like to think of an ending yourself?

Did you like the multiplication game?

Write about your books, what you are doing at school, about your friends; write about Dima and Mama.

I embrace both my sons,
Papa

13. *To his Wife and Sons*

My darling!

Dima and Lesik – hello!

Today I won't be able to write to all of you, only to Mama.

I've received your twelfth letter so far. Your letters are so good for me. Just what I need. It's a pity that I can't answer you as I should like to.

I don't know if you've had any letters from me and if you have, which ones. So once again I'll have to touch upon a purely practical matter.

I should like you, Mother and Ada, to share between you the visits allowed me, and to come and see me regularly. It's already been a week since I've seen any of you. If it's a question of money, then spend less on the parcels.

Now, about the parcels. Don't waste so much money on delicacies. Meat, cheese, butter. I don't need sugar at the moment. The fruit must be something that doesn't rot quickly. I loved the honey-cakes. But cakes aren't necessary in general. As for the rest – please yourself, you know best. I don't need garlic for the time being. Only do come to a proper agreement with Mother – about both the visits and the parcels.

On your next visit (or in a parcel) let me have a pair of hospital pyjamas (warm ones) and some tooth-powder.

I've had letters from Seryozha Borshchevsky and Sasha Feldman.* I'm sending a letter to Tamara and Sasha, through

* Kiev friends of Plyushch, co-authors of an appeal on his behalf referred to below, p. 114. Feldman, a human rights and pro-Zionist activist, was arrested in November 1973 and later sentenced on a trumped-up charge to three and a half years of forced labour. *Tr.*

Vladik.* To economise on envelopes, I'm sending a number of letters through you.

You saw what state of mind I was in. In essence, nothing has changed in this respect. Last Sunday I sent you a fairy tale (in the form of an 'introduction') for Lesik – about a reed-mouse. I'm planning one more instalment. Let me know, honestly, how he reacted to it (and about your own reaction – although I don't pretend to the slightest measure of literary talent. I, unfortunately, simply can't think up a plot, and without a plot it's not a story, only a zoological fantasy). I should really like to write something that would interest them both. I still can't get hold of what I wrote earlier. And conditions are not favourable for composing anything new.

I'll be able to reply to Dima, in answer to his revealing letters and your own letters about him. You write so well about him, in such detail. Go on writing like that about him.

You're a wonder – writing every day. But I think that you won't have enough strength to keep that up for long, and so it would be better for you to write less often, but systematically. Your letters – and everyone else's – are very precious to me. And if I don't answer all of them, or if I'm very brief in my replies, the explanation lies in my state of mind and in my present circumstances.

I've already read most of what you have given me. I'm reading Shchedrin at the moment; I've read the Bunin† volume. That is not quite the appropriate kind of literature for me. All that immemorial, ancestral, languorous nostalgia and melancholy, going on and on. It depresses me, and that is no help at all.

I've just re-read your letters. I can picture for myself quite clearly all the changes you have made, everything you've done around the house. I can't think of all this going on without me.

I should like Dima to share his impressions of Odessa with me, and Lesik his view of Tashkent (from your account). Only, you mustn't make them write.

* V. Nedobora. *Tr.*

† I. A. Bunin (1870–1953), a Russian aristocrat *émigré* writer and Nobel Prize winner. Some of his works have recently been published in the USSR. *Tr.*

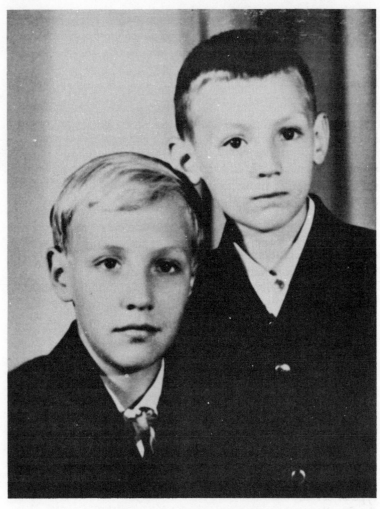

Dima (left) and Lesik Plyushch.

And now, about your letters.

Dima, I'm so glad that you've been helping Lesik with his work.

And Lesik, you're a good boy, listening to Dima and loving him. By the way, Dima, read the Goncourt Brothers' *Zemganno Brothers*. It describes the kind of friendship between brothers that I should like you two to have.

How is your new acquaintance, the little boy from Polesye? Has he come to see you yet? It was a lovely story.

I don't really know about the motor-cycle. I don't have anything against it, but you know more about it. If he's going to earn the money for it himself, it would help him to think more seriously when making plans for the future.

As for the art school, let Dima make up his own mind about it. Vova's arguments in favour of the school are quite convincing.

I still haven't adapted myself properly to my surroundings. That's why I m so emotionally tense compared with my Kiev period. But you, my dearest – you keep on writing as you have been doing up to now.

I'll send you some notes I'm making on the various books I'm reading. Perhaps they will be of real use to me as well at some later date. Other quotations are of use only to myself.

'Words have souls. Most readers, and even writers, search only for their meaning. But one must discover their soul, which emerges in the relation of each word with other words, which erupts in some books and floods them with an unknown light; yet it is a fire in words which is difficult to extinguish' (Maupassant). This is on the subject of the strange nature of artistic communication, which bears no resemblance to the ordinary, commonsense type of communication. I hope, all the same, to do some work in the future on the psychology of emotion, which interested me so much over the question of games.

That's all for now, my darling.

Greetings to my friends.

Your Lyonya

9.9.73

I'm sending a letter to Sasha Feldman and Seryozha in this envelope. Please forward it to them.

14. *To Viktor Sharapov*

My dear friend, Viktor!

I was very happy to get your letter. Tanya wrote to me about your letters, so I knew you hadn't disappeared without trace, and that means that we shall meet again some day.

It's a pity that we spent such a short time together. I was on good terms with all my cell-mates, but I only established a real friendship with you. It was strange, how I liked you 'at first sight'. The only time this has happened to me before was when I first met Tanya.

It's good to know that you're writing to her, and let me say a big 'thank you' for the birthday present you sent her. I'm quite sad that I haven't any sort of talent, with which I could make her a present. I did think up some games for my sons, but I don't know whether they liked them.

Tanya will write to you in more detail about my state of mind here. I wouldn't say I was feeling very hale and hearty. Due to the medicine I am given, I sleep most of the time – day and night – and I walk around as if I were under water.

Tanya sends me books. I read them, and sometimes make notes. I've had to abandon my scientific studies, and that is perhaps what I feel worst about at present.

Write about yourself. Why didn't you write anything at all about yourself? I myself know that one can't think of anything to write about oneself. And, as far as I am concerned, there's also my condition, under treatment. What are your hopes, and the actual possibilities, of getting home? How long do you have to wait?

As for holding on – I am holding on, and I think that I can endure whatever happens. As regards 'the pleasures of this life' that you write about, to be honest, I am beginning to have my doubts about those. What kind of pleasures. . . . That this is an education – yes, I agree. It is – as is the whole of life. However, I should have preferred not to have had to attend some of the classes in that 'school of life', but one can't look a gift horse in the mouth.

Write to Dima, please, about the method of fishing that you

described to me – 'float-fishing'. I've forgotten the sizes and other details.

I'll end here, for the time being.

Do keep writing, though I fear that any interesting letters would not reach me.

I send you a really friendly greeting.

Yours,

L. Plyushch

2.9.73

15. *To two Friends, a Husband and Wife*

My dear Toma* and Sasha!

It is not by accident that your names are put in that order. According to our Ukrainian custom, a husband's natural place is under the heel of his better half. I share that lot, too, and am in full compliance with the arrangement. Judging by your letter, it would seem that Sasha is trying to get the reins of authority into his own hands, and even ascribes to himself child-bearing functions: 'Tamara and I have managed to get married and bear a child.' 'We have toiled together!'

Julia Aleksandrovna has already praised your new arrival to me, and although I personally have always regarded such tiny morsels of humanity with some misgiving – and I think that Sasha, too, may be feeling no positive emotions towards him (?) – I'm very happy to congratulate you, Toma, on having Boris. Sasha will, of course, get to like the feeling of fatherhood in due course. Or are you an exception?

Having shared in your most important event, let me now go on to secondary matters. Wait, though – I was forgetting about Daniel. You wrote about him so vaguely, Sasha; do write more precisely. How did he arrive, and why, etc. I'm afraid to say something stupid when referring to this. I'd be interested to hear what Toma has to say about it.

It's difficult for me to judge a book by its title, so I don't really know whether it would be worth while reading *The Apology of*

---

* Clearly the same as Tamara, mentioned above. *Tr.*

History. Consult Tanya about it. I read a lot here – whatever Tanya sends me.

On reading Toma's letter I realized more clearly who Daniel is. In that case I'm very happy for you, happy on two counts.

Why do you think that I can't find it interesting to torment you with the help of Freud? Or do you think he doesn't make sense? At first reading, none of them make much sense. I think Sasha is more interested in Daniel at the moment.

I've had a letter from Vladik, from Kharkov. I finally answered it today. I've already explained to everyone why I find it hard to answer letters, so I won't repeat it again.

Unfortunately, I don't know who among you has received any of my letters. I'm under the impression that even Tanya hasn't yet received any of them.

How long will Daniel be staying with you? If he's staying for a long time, I'd be interested to know how you're going to bring him up. Try to keep a diary on both of them – two or three sentences a day. Daniel is just starting on his period of learning to play games: you can watch him and give him a lot of help. Try to assist his development by means of games. I am perfectly convinced that there are great possibilities in education through games. Going by Sasha's character ('anal-sadistic'), you could expect a liking for systematization, constructive-building games, lotto and matching pictures, cut-out pictures. But you must also rely on subject-role games (in particular) and generic games.

I shall try and write in more detail about all this after I have received your reply.

Well, goodbye for now; I shall sit and read Shchedrin, which Tanya has sent me.

Yours,

Lyonya

6.9.73

16. *To his Elder Son, Dima*

My dear son,

I've received your letter, with your answers to my questions and the extracts from a journal. I'm just glancing through *Technology for the Young*, as I've already read these same articles. But keep on sending me extracts – just take them from other journals. I see that you have wide interests. I shall be able to debate with you on any subjects you may like to touch upon – so that I'll know exactly what you find interesting. Do you read *Around the World*?* I've read a number of issues – found them very interesting. On history, have you read *Riddles of History* (we have it at home) and Ceram's *Gods, Graves and Scholars*? I didn't like history at school, as I happened to have teachers who were no good at teaching it. Now I regret this, as my knowledge of history is, consequently, weak. So I often have to refrain from taking part in discussions. I perceived that you have given up learning to draw, from your drawings themselves. They are good, but it's obvious that you haven't progressed much.

You write that the letter which I wrote to you from Kiev, about sophistry, would have been interesting. I shall try to recall what I then said, at least in part. I won't be able to manage a complete recapitulation, as I need to be in the right frame of mind for that (here we have the first link between thought and feeling – for effective thought, an appropriate emotional state is necessary, especially for what we call inspiration).

In this letter I'll begin with Greek sophistry, and, in my next letter, I'll go on to the Sophists' 'pupils', yourself in particular (Mama writes that you still haven't abandoned this style of argument).

The Sophists of ancient Greece made their appearance at the point of time when it was being realized that words could be used equally successfully either to defend, or to prove, completely (diametrically) opposite statements. For example, the philosopher Heraclitus proved that everything in the world is in a state of perpetual motion and change, that nothing stands still or is

* Popular Soviet travel magazine. *Tr.*

permanent. The philosopher Protagoras proved the opposite – that changes in the world are not real changes, that they have no real significance. And indeed, we see that anything, any phenomenon eventually changes and disappears, that everything is in a state of motion. But Protagoras is also right: from the fact that summer turns into autumn, autumn into winter, and so on, we can only conclude that this change is no change at all, repeating itself, as it does, year after year. People die, but a new generation replaces the old – everything repeats itself. It's true, isn't it, that clearly they are both right.

The Sophists thought up many interesting paradoxes. For instance, the arrow that never eached its target, or Heracles not being able to overtake a tortoise (ask Mama to tell you about these).

The paradoxes of the Sophists, or sophisms, arose either because of a wrong proof (a mistake in logic), or as a result of insufficient scientific knowledge.

In my view, the Sophists have proved very useful, in spite of the fact that they often used their arguments for unworthy ends.

They made people examine their way of thinking and their methods of verification, and so they helped to found the science of thinking – logic. They also showed that, in nature, nothing is as simple as it looks. Many phenomena have to be thought about for a long time, before they can be explained.

The Sophists' main defect was their dishonest, biased way of thinking: proofs and arguments were produced, not in order to get at the truth, but so as to beat their opponents' arguments by all possible means. This, incidentally, is also characteristic of most children when arguing – they argue not to find out the truth but to show that they themselves are right (but I'll discuss that next time). This leads to the development of a wrong, dishonest form of thinking. In science – real science – honest, unbiased thinking is absolutely essential.

In debate, it's important to listen to your opponent's arguments, to find out what he may be right about. The sophistical method of argument tries to discover only the mistakes in an opponent's standpoint, paying no attention to any faults in their own argument which the opponent may have uncovered. This is where the dishonesty of their thinking comes to light.

As literally anything can be proved by the appropriate use of words (by quibbling about words, by twisting them), then it follows that proof must be based on practical demonstration alone. I call practical demonstration 'the argument of Diogenes'. When the philosopher Diogenes had got tired of listening to someone trying to prove that motion does not exist, he began walking round and round his opponent until the opponent was annoyed. In this way Diogenes had, in practice, got his opponent to recognize the existence of motion (i.e. of his movement).

Carefully observe your own arguments with your mother. I think you will often realize that you are, in fact, wrong, that in practice Mama is quite right, yet you go on arguing by simply juggling with words.

I should also like to draw your attention to the following point. One single mistake allowed in your thinking is quite enough to enable you to prove, subsequently, whatever you like on that basis. Here's an example of a sophism, built upon such a mistake.

Let's prove that God exists.

Definition: God is an intelligent being, identical with the universe.

Theorem 1. To prove that $1 = 2$.

$$1 - 2 \times 1 \times 3/2 + 9/4 = 4 - 2 \times 2 \times 3/2 + 9/4$$

– this equation is the equation of the square of the differences.

$$(1 - 3/2)^2 = (2 - 3/2)^2$$

Let's take the square root of the two sides.

$1 - 3/2 = 2 - 3/2$. Therefore
$1 = 2$; which is what we wanted to prove.

Theorem 2. To prove that any number is equal to any other number.

If $1 = 2$, then $0 = 1$ (carry 1 over to the right side). Multiply both sides any number of times ($\times A$). $0 = A$. Which means that any number A is equal to 0. Which means that B also equals 0.

We'll write it like this: $0 = A$
$$B = 0$$

Put both equations together:

$$0 + B = A + 0$$

Therefore $A = B$, and A and B can be any number. Which is what we wanted to prove.

Theorem 3. God exists.
Let there be N number of intelligent beings and M number of unintelligent (or even non-living) beings in the world. As any number is equal to any other number, then $N = 1$, and $M = 0$. Which means the whole world is equal to one intelligent being. Which is what we wanted to prove.

Try and find a mistake in this sophism.

The practical 'argument of Diogenes' disproves Theorem 1. This removes the basis of the whole argument. The rest is all correct. Obviously, using Theorem 1, you could prove anything.

As regards the third theorem, you may object: why should N be equal to 1, and not, for example, to 3? Quite right. But that would only prove that God was both one and three. And, in fact, that is exactly what some religions assert.

I write to you in such detail about sophisms because I notice in you a dangerous tendency to sophistical argument.

If you want to be educated, then it is obviously most important for you to fight that tendency.

I'll stop here. Write to me about books, about yourself and Lesik, about everything.

Papa

17. *To Leonid Plyushch from his Younger Son, Lesik*
Dear Papa!

You have always been the dearest person in the world for me, and you still are. I liked your story about the Reed-mouse very much, and in this letter I'm going to tell you what I want to happen in it next. I want the Reed-mouse to go to the land of the letter-eaters and become ill there, and for them to heal him with 'bitter truth', and then he can go to the land of technology, and then he could fly back in a flying machine made by Vintik and Shpunktik. And he would fly home to his own pond.

I went to the cinema and saw the film 'Ivan Vassilievich changes his job', and I saw another film 'Parade, forward!'. I liked both films. 'Ivan Vassilievich changes his job' was about a time machine, and you will have probably guessed who Ivan Vassilievich was. He was Ivan the Fourth, the Terrible Tsar; in the film he comes to the twentieth century from his own time. But you will be asking, no doubt, who invented the time machine? In the film it was invented by someone you probably know – Shurik.

And 'Parade, forward!' is about a circus, there were a lot of interesting acts shown in this film, but there weren't any acts like sword-swallowing or an acrobat walking on red-hot coals in bare feet.

Go on writing the story about the Reed-mouse.

Dear Papa, goodbye until the next letter.

× × × × × × × ×

I liked your story very much. And I liked the Reed-mouse Dimle, too. Most of all I liked the bit where the Reed-mouse Dimle played on the reed as if it was a flute. I liked everything about the Reed-mouse and how Dimle played with the sunbeams. Now I should like to know about Dimle's travels and how he found other reed-mice, and how they lived in their reed-land, one in the reed-land and another in Dimle-land, and they would call that land 'Dimle-land' because Dimle discovered it.

I like the second-year class very much, because we learn Ukrainian and nature study.

I saw elk traces in the forest, and I even saw wild-boar tracks.

I was in Tashkent as well, and I saw camels, mules, and the old bazaar, where there were many huge melons and water-melons.

I am very sad without you and I wish you could come home sooner.

× × × × × × × ×

My dear Papa!

It's very boring without you. Do write some stories and rhymes and some more pieces about the 'letter-eaters'.

Papa, I have a microscope, and I have already seen many interesting things through it. For example, I saw such tiny insects that you can't see them with your eyes alone.

Papa, I was in Odessa. Aunt Ada and I caught some crabs there. I didn't catch any crabs myself, of course, but I did catch two sea-urchins. Dima and I have already got our flippers. We swam in them.

Papa, write to us more often. I love you very much.

Your son Lesik Plyushch

18. *To his Wife*

My fairy-tale!

Why I call you my fairy-tale will not, unfortunately, be clear to you. In one of my letters from Kiev I tried to explain my concept of the 'fairy-tale life', basing myself on Prishvin's 'Root of Life', Grin's* 'Scarlet Sails', on Schiller and so on. We see the fairy-tale in life by gazing into life (and discovering its essential meaning) or we search for it, or create it.

But I can't recreate the mood I was in when I wrote that, and so I won't try to reconstruct the letter. I tried to recreate my letter to Dima about sophistical thinking. And it wasn't a success. It came out dry and incomplete. Write to me about his true reaction to it. Because, judging by his letters, he may be writing to me diplomatically, to spare my feelings.

To my regret, I received only one letter this week, from Dima. There weren't any from you. So today I'm only going to write about the books. Write and tell me when you sent the parcel and when you received notification that I had received it. The parcel has obviously been delayed in the post. I'm reading *The Philosophy of Art* at the moment. I've read Bakhtin on 'The problem of Dostoyevsky's poetry'. I shall write down some excerpts which are to some extent related to my own ideas. While I was still in Moscow I had begun to study the psychological nature of humour. My aim was this: to explain the structure of witticisms and, after isolating this aspect, to go on to the psychological

---

* *A. Grin* – the pen-name of A. S. Grinevsky (1880–1932), Russian writer of fantasies. *Tr.*

aspect. Luk has done much to explain the structural side. I wrote to Tatyana Sergeyevna about my theory that the word 'humour' is etymologically connected with the word '*mort*' – death, and that this shows a distinct psychological link between the fear of death (and other emotions connected with death) and laughter, the origin of laughter. I have now discovered that 'humour' comes from '*humor*', which means moisture, or liquid. But I still hope to succeed in establishing the link between '*amour*', 'humour' and '*mort*'.

'Over the centuries, the carnival has been a great conscious experience for the people throughout the world. This conscious experience expresses freedom from fear, and brings man closer to other men and to the world as a whole.' And the main point of carnivals is laughter.

'Everything has its parody, i.e. its laughable aspect, for everything is resurrected and renewed through death. In Rome, the laughter of the parody was a necessary part of both funerals and triumphs.'

I found indirect support for my ideas on riddles (which I have written to you about) in Vygotsky: 'In riddles, it is precisely the distancing of the image used from the meaning it is supposed to express, that is necessary for the achievement of the riddle's poetic effect. . . . Compare this with the way in which teachers – who wanted to replace the wise, but difficult, folk-riddles with rational riddles that would stimulate the development of children's thought processes – set insipid riddles to the children, such as the following: what stands in a corner and sweeps the room? Answer – the broom. This riddle is a typical example, in that it depends entirely on graphic description and rationalisation, and is completely lacking in poetic effect.'

Have you read *The Psychology of Art*? It's a difficult book, but it contains a great many interesting ideas on various subjects of general interest.

I send you a big kiss,* as Mother always writes,

Your Lyonya Greetings to everyone

---

* A pun. What his mother wrote was 'Ts.K.' – '*Tseluyu Krepko*' ('I send you a big kiss') but the same initials usually stand for the 'Central Committee' (of the Communist Party). *Tr.*

19. *To his Wife*

My darling!

I've received your twentieth letter. Haven't you got mixed up? Shouldn't it be the nineteenth?

I've had two letters this week – one from you and one from Ada. I'm answering them in turn.

I'm glad Lesik liked the beginning of my story. But unfortunately, I can't seem to get down to writing the next instalment. I feel the plot is very weak. The next part should be about a small boy, who opens the 'singing reed' and tries to discover why it sings. There should be some kind of plot, and a conclusion, but I don't feel able to produce anything at the moment. If he asks about it, explain that I'm busy (or give some other reason). I should so much like to keep up a correspondence with both of them. But how? What can I write about?

Ada writes that when Lesik is with her and Mother he doesn't whine as much as he does when he's with you. The reason is obvious: at home, he's under conditions that he's been used to since his pre-school days, he has a standardized relationship with you, or more exactly (in structuralistic terms), a relationship that has become a habit. You'll have to change this habit somehow, otherwise it will become second nature for him (to whine and complain when he's with his immediate relatives, and control himself when he's with other people).

I'm following my old ideas here, on the rational aspect of the Oedipus complex. I think that in his early years, especially in a family environment, a child develops relationships of various kinds – with his father, his mother, his grandfather and grandmother, his brothers, etc. (with all the active members of his family). These kinds of relationship are distorted and applied to other people. Independent relationship lines are formed: the father's line, the mother's, the brother's, and so on (apart from their emotional significance, their 'role' in childhood).

This sort of line can be clearly found in Shevchenko, in Dostoyevsky, and in quite insignificant writers as well. The structure of images in the work of this or that writer is often (if not always) grouped along certain lines.

For example, Shevchenko has a line linking 'Christ' and 'the orphan'. ranging from the author's 'I' through Gont, the Decembrists, Christ, Prometheus. . . . What lies behind the 'I'? Or is this in fact the line of the 'I' relationship?

Freud's mistake, I feel, was to divide relationships into two lines (father/mother), besides which he took individual instances of a 'cliché-type' relationship as expressing a general rule, and therefore made the whole relationship too sexual in character.

I'm now reading Vygotsky's *Thought and Speech*. Have you read it? Look through the introduction by Leontyev and Lurie* carefully. It contains some passages you could find useful. If you like, I could send you excerpts from it, which I've made notes on for myself, and commented on in connection with games.

You haven't written anything about the multiplication game for Lesik. In connection with it, I've made a note of the following passage in Vygotsky: 'The motives for learning to write do not really mean anything yet to a child starting to learn to write. Apart from that, as in all new forms of activity, the motivation for speech, the need for speech precedes the development of that activity. That motivation precedes activity is true not only when applied to ontogenetics, but also as regards every conversation, every phrase.'

The motive – 'I must do this to learn it properly' – is often insufficient, not only for first-year schoolchildren, but even for much older children. In particular, a child feels no necessity to learn multiplication. A game, of the kind I sent to you, gives a motivation for each step, each act of multiplication. This is a motivation derived from the game ('I want to play I want to win, and for that I must be able to multiply correctly.' I can't remember whether I included in the rules that if the multiplication is incorrect, a move is missed).

You could make use of this in your work. This concept is related to a more common one: 'A thought is not its own final authority.' A thought does not, in itself, originate from another thought, but from the motivating sphere of our consciousness,

---

* *Aleksey Nikolayevich Leontyev* (born 1903) and probably *Aleksey Romanovich Lurie* (born 1902), both psychologists. *Tr.*

which encompasses our needs and inclinations, our interests and motives, our aberrations and emotions. Behind our thoughts are assertive and volitional tendencies. I've already written about the links between thought and emotion. It's important, at this point, to underline the pre-eminently emotional character of game-playing, the emotional fulfilment provided by the playing of games – exactly what is needed for the birth of thought.

I don't think I need 'Conflicting Structures'. Give me more details – what is it about? In my situation, I find it difficult even to read Vygotsky (it's hard to concentrate), and it's obvious that I could have no success in reading mathematical books. So that it is worth while my reading a mathematical book only if it completely corresponds with my interests.

Now, Bakhtin* makes splendid reading. But I fear that you may be wasting too much on me, that you won't be able to read as much yourself. For example, you need Vygotsky more than I do.

Someone has managed to send me a large sum of money, and I now have 80 roubles altogether. Why ever have you done this? In any case I won't be able to spend that much. Please don't waste so much money on me.

I have not yet received either your parcel or Sasha's (which he sent, from Averintsev). Meat products should be the tendency for parcels.

Leaving these practical matters aside, let me return to the question of reading. I've read a few issues of *Around the World*. This journal has become somewhat better than *Science and Life*. Dima! I advise you to read it regularly. It contains many interesting articles on popular science – observations, stories, including science-fiction. I enjoyed reading almost all the articles in it.

Did Sasha Feldman get my letter? If not, then thank him for the very nice card he sent me (and, naturally, for the books as well).

Lotman's book was published in 1972 (or was it '71?). Have you seen it anywhere?

It's a pity that things have turned out so stupidly. When I was

* *Mikhail Bakhtin* (died 1975), Soviet literary scholar. *Tr.*

engaged in studying games, I didn't have the right books; now I have the books, but I can't make use of them.

This, in brief, is what I have managed to do in a year and a half. I've finished the draft of 'Morphology of the Game', or – to be more precise – 'The Structure and Typology of Intellectual Games'. 'The emotional balance of intellectual games' is in thesis form, together with my work on some other types of games. I have made some progress on the didactic aspect of games, on 'self-sufficiency' and on 'objectivisation–disobjectivisation' in games, on calibration in game systems, on 'The important role of games in the development of the pre-school-age child'. I have written an article on 'The game as a specific form of reflection', and I've planned a thesis to add to the article on games which are modelled on the world-view of the ancients (like the model of time in '*nardy*' and '*guski*'). By the way, you appear to have forgotten to send me Gurvich's article (?) on time – it was one of my basic sources.

I'm especially sorry about not having this article. There are in it some very unexpected deductions. It should perhaps have been included in the Tartu collection. Its more interesting deductions are concerned with 'emotional balance in the game', with 'objectivization', and 'self-sufficiency'. These themes develop into whole theories, which agree, on the one hand, with Vygotsky (in *Psychology of Art* and in his articles on games), and, on the other hand, with the 'Philosophic–Economic Manuscripts' and Batishchev's articles on objectivization. I've asked Genchik and Vladik to send me the latter.

Could you possibly try asking if I could be allowed to have my papers (for a short time only) so that I could copy out my basic propositions. Then I could at least go on thinking about those subjects and, in particular, I could exchange various views on games with you, in the form of propositions.

I've by now abandoned the hope of doing any work on Shevchenko and humour.

I'll stop now. Until next time.

Your Lyonya

22.9.73

P.S. I've continued the story, somewhat uncertainly. Write and tell me his reaction. By the way, if the magic formula of 'Sikle' is not clear, explain to him (Lesik) that it can turn to sound 'Le-sik'. But let him try – tell him so – to guess it for himself.

In the time I have left, I'll write out a few excerpts from books.

'However, what one cannot agree with at all is his idealization of the psychology of love, and because of this trait he belongs to that group of writers who transform human emotion by their art.' (Maupassant on Pierre Loti. I read some Loti in Lefortovo prison. Maupassant's analysis is quite correct.) This agrees quite well with the basic ideas of Tolstoy and Markov about the social function of literature (art) being the transformation of emotion.

'How many women there must be, who don't know me, and for whom I don't yet exist!' (Flaubert's *Don Juan*.) What a wonderful expression of the link between love and the loneliness of the subject! This is what I was discussing with you on our last evening together (from Mark Twain's Autobiography): 'Before the spelling-book came with its arbitrary forms, men unconsciously revealed shades of their characters, and also added enlightening shades of expression to what they wrote, by their spelling.' Very similar ideas are formulated scientifically by Vygostky – on formal and comprehensive grammar.

20. *To his Younger Son*

My dear, good, Lesik!

I'm very glad that you liked the beginning of my story. Now I'm sending you the next part. Write and tell me if you like it. I myself like the beginning better.

The Singing Reed

Early one morning, a small boy went to the pond in which Dimle was living in his reed-house. He was a very ordinary little boy, not at all like people in fairy tales. Only his name, Sikle, had something a little magical about it. But nobody knew this – not even Sikle himself. At this point somebody's sure to say 'What's in a name?' Well, that's not quite true. Try it out for yourself. Repeat the name over and over again, very quickly – 'Sikle –

Sikle – Sikle' – and you'll see for yourself what the magic was in the little boy's name.

He had one other unusual quality – he was very, very inquisitive. Whatever he heard about, or saw, interested him at once, and he tried to investigate it or explore it.

One evening Sikle heard that, every morning, a choir of male frogs could be heard singing 'The Song of the Sun' on the banks of the neighbouring pond. And, of course, he immediately asked his mother and father to wake him up early on the following morning, so that he could see the frogs' choir for himself.

Even before he had reached the pond, Sikle caught sight of the first frog. It was hopping unhurriedly towards the pond. Sikle followed it carefully, hoping it would lead him to the meeting-place of the whole choir.

Suddenly a slight wind blew up. And then Sikle heard soft music. He listened attentively and intently. The sound was coming from the direction of the pond. 'The frog choir', thought Sikle, and he followed the frog even more carefully. It reached the bank, looked round, stared at Sikle, and jumped into the water. Sikle walked all round the pond – the music was coming from all over it.

But however carefully he looked among the reeds and into the water, he could not see any singers. What is more, this did not sound like the usual sort of frog concert. It was more like instrumental music than singing.

Sikle was so deep in thought about the mysterious music that he didn't notice a twig in front of him, and he stepped on it. There was a loud snap. But the music did not stop. 'Which means it can't be frogs. They'd have been frightened by the noise and would have hidden themselves. The wind is blowing in the direction of the pond. Perhaps it's bringing the musical sound with it.' And Sikle started walking towards the direction the wind was blowing from. The music grew fainter.

Sikle realized he had been wrong again – the music was indeed coming from the pond.

By the time he got back to the side of the pond, the music had stopped altogether. The wind had also died away. After standing for a while by the pond, pondering about it all, Sikle came to the conclusion that the music had something to do with the wind. When the wind died down, the music fainted away; when the wind blew stronger, the music grew louder. 'Which means it's made by the wind', Sikle finally decided. The puzzle grew more and more mysterious. 'But how can the wind make music, and by what means? By blowing through the reed-stems or leaves? No – they only rustle.'

Sikle took a closer look at the reeds, and only then did he notice that the reeds in this pond were very strange – they were full of holes. 'So that's where the music is coming from! Someone has turned the reeds into reed-pipes.'

You've already guessed – haven't you? – what was happening at the pond?

When Dimle had played to his heart's content on his reed-house-pipe, he climbed on to his roof-brush, right up to its very top. The wind bent the reed, and the brush bent down, leaning on to the top of a neighbouring reed. Dimle jumped across on to that reed. And at that moment he had a great idea – to turn the whole reed-bed into a choir. 'No sooner thought of, than done', is every reed-mouse's motto.

The reed-mouse gnawed holes in the stem of each reed, one by one, climbing to the feathery top of one reed and jumping on to the next reed-house. He did this in the same way as little boys swing from tree to tree in a dense forest. They climb to the top of a slender, springy tree. Through the weight of their bodies, the tree sways, bending downwards. By clinging to the thinnest branches, the boys slide down the boughs to the ground, as if on sledge runners.

But Dimle was so small and light that he always had to wait for the wind to help him bend the reed. One, two – a leap – and he landed on the leaves of the neighbouring reed-house. A second leap – and he was on the roof-brush of the second reed-house. A third leap, and – he was in the water. 'Brrr – how cold it is! I'll have to go up to the roof and dry myself in the sun.'

And so, a few hours later, the pool had become a musical pool. A passer-by heard the music, saw the beautiful frog, and decided that he was the singer. But he was wrong, because he was unobservant.

Sikle pulled up a few of the reeds – but found nothing in them. The mystery of the Musical Pond became the mystery of who had made the holes in the reeds.

What was he to do? Pull up all the reeds?

He could solve the mystery that way but, if he did so, the Musical Pond would be no more.

Sikle stayed by the pond until it was time for lunch, but he still did not solve the mystery.

That evening he brought his mother, father and brother down to the pond. They heard a number of pieces of music, but they could not guess how it was done.

21. *To his Wife*

Good-morning, my fairy-tale!

This week I've received a lot of letters. Numbers 26–27 and 23 from you. Letters from Julia A., from Verkhman* and from Seryozha. I have not had any letters from Klara. Tell her to write again. Seryozha has sent me his translations of Lorca. Pass on my reply to him.

I can't really judge the quality of the translation. I liked the poems and the translation into Ukrainian (that is, I don't have any comments to make on the quality of the language). But I find it difficult to reply to such a letter – full of poetry. Seryozha, if those had been your own poems, I would have ventured an opinion. But try to understand my difficulty in finding a theme to write on.

For the same reason I can't really write to Slava. Give him my regards. But I think that he will find it as difficult to write as I do.

Now I'll turn to your own letter.

What kind of fruit and vegetables are you trying to bring? I've already said that these shouldn't be too hard (hard apples, carrots, radishes) nor fast-decaying foodstuffs (to be more precise, such things as grapes, soft plums, etc., should only be in small quantities). You can bring nuts. It's not worth bringing sweets. Chocolates and halva are all right. I've noticed a general tendency

* Kiev friend of Plyushch, co-author of appeal. See p. 114. *Tr.*

towards sweet things in what you've been bringing. Some of the patients have small tins of cooked meats sent to them – smoked meat, sausage, etc. Bring some ham and cheese.

But that's quite enough of that. I'm satisfied with anything you bring me. You yourself decide what it's to be. For instance, that cake was something I could never have expected. You are quite right: it is good to remember the art of making presents.

You write about your inner conversations with me. Here, I have consciously put an end to my own inner conversations with you – so as to avoid deepening my longing for you, for our home, our children and friends. This is reflected in my letters. When I was in Kiev, I wrote you long, emotional letters.

Whenever I start reading literary works – they permeate into my letters. I've already written to you about how much I enjoyed Prishvin. Could you buy 'Root of Life' and 'Drop of Water' (also 'Phatselia'),* both for yourself and for me? Why haven't you said anything about these books in your letters? I've already written to you about them. I'd especially like to express my feelings for you with the help of Prishvin's images. My own words and images are not to my satisfaction. If you read these works, notice the image of the deer which turns into a princess. In 'Phatselia' and 'Root of Life' ('*Zhen-shen*') this is reinforced by other images. Taken as a whole, these express the concept of love as a myth or fairy-tale (or more broadly, as a 'taming'), the realization of life as a fairy-tale. In a similar way, we give children's scrawls meaning by raising them to the rank of meaningful drawings (the meaning springs up anew and then begins to influence the form – the 'scrawls' gradually really change into drawings, appropriate to the meaning). So, in creating a fairy-tale which represents actual biological relationships, we humanize and spiritualize them, raising them to a new level. The establishment of biological relationships on a new, magic level of meaning transforms them into human relationships – love, friendship, and so on. This also involves, partly, the 'taming' of objects – the emergence of a human relationship to inanimate objects.

I once spoke to you about this new concept – the human

* Herbal plant (Lat. *phacelia*) which grows in North America and Mexico. *Tr.*

concept of love (the overcoming of loneliness by the individual). 'Phatselia' contains some beautiful passages expressing the 'extension of the self', as Prishvin puts it. It's a pity I don't have the book by me. There's a great deal in it on the substitution of the entire world as a single being for the image of a lost love. Read both stories – and I think you will then understand what my own feelings were while I was reading them.

The transformation of the deer into a princess corresponds to the story of the frog-princess – the transformation comes about under the influence of the love-myth. The myth, or fairy tale, is shown to possess real life-giving power. This is yet another aspect of the theme of life as a fairy tale, and the taming of life. (The taming of the deer marks the revelation of the princess within it.) It's difficult to explain this more clearly, without falling back on artistic imagery.

The whole concept is based first and foremost on the transformation of the 'scrawl of life' into the fairy-tale of life, the actual story of the magic of love, 'love's image', under the influence of an established fairy-tale structure and a change in perception, to encompass the magic. Whatever new meaning we introduce into actual relationships becomes part of them (if the original proposition is workable. In any case, some change in that direction will take place. An idea superimposed on reality changes it, through reality adapting itself to the idea.)

If you get me that book I'll be able to explain it all much better, more clearly – by commenting on and interpreting Prishvin.

Have you seen the translation of the 'Gospel of Thomas' in the anthology *Ancient and Modern*? It's of a much lower standard than the canonical Gospels, both in form and in content. Nevertheless, I was glad of the opportunity to read it. It arouses thought, and feeling.

Indeed in that volume I found a number of pieces which were of interest to me. One supplemented Gurvich's* article on time, another was about the concept of comedy in ancient times, and

* See page 15, footnote.

then there was that piece by Averintsev.* Taken in its entirety, however, the book is somewhat specialized, only for philologists in fact.

Your report on the introduction of 'education through games' among six-year-olds in Georgia really interested me. Send me everything you come across about this. As long as it is not over-done, as regards the educational aspect, there will be no terrible consequences for those six-year-olds at school. This somewhat resembles Sukhomlinsky's 'zero class' or his idea of education through games and stories.

Your question about games of classification caught me unpre-pared. I have not studied this very much, so I really can't add anything new. Put your questions in a more concrete form, describe your own work and your theses, and then I may be able to add something myself.

Goodbye for now, my darling.

Hallo there, Dima and Lesik! How are you? How are things at school? Write to me about yourselves in more detail.

14.10.73

I can't understand where J. A. has got to – she wrote to me from the Crimea, but the letter came from Kharkov. So I'm sending you a letter for her. You can read it, too, by the way – I explain the idea of the fairy-tale better to her. Send her my thanks for the postcards as well. I forgot to include that.

I won't be able to write a letter in reply to Sasha today. Send them both a greeting from me.

22. *To a Friend*

Dear Julia Alexandrovna,

Everyone seems to have agreed together to write to me about Lesik. Tanya, and my sister, and Tatyana Sergeyevna, and you yourself. Of course, it was all very pleasant to read. I would be very glad if some of the praise about Lesik could be transferred to Dima. I hope that, in spite of many traits in his character, Dima will grow up to be not at all a bad person.

As for Lesik, it is quite amazing to what high degree all of my

* A Moscow scholar. *Tr.*

own tendencies and interests are reproduced in him (in the Freudian sense. He has exactly the same kind of mentality as myself). So I may assume that all his faults of character will, to some extent, also be the same as mine. I feel that his collections and his aptitude for collecting things ought to be given a deeper meaning, so that he doesn't remain stuck at that level (the 'hoarding' stage). His thinking should be developed through comprehension. For example, he has a collection of sea-shells. He could now be encouraged to 'investigate' the way in which the spiral lines on the shells curl. Do they all appear to curl to the left? Are there none that curl to the right? Give him an aim – to find some like that. Is there any other difference in those that curl to the right? I write all this at random, as my knowledge on this subject is more than weak. You yourself must be much better at finding such problems, that he can try and solve.

Our kind of mentality is always in danger of leaping superficially from one problem to another or, more exactly, from one subject to another, as the point of study consists precisely in proceeding from superficial investigation of mysteries to a problematical approach to reality. He and I are lovers of mysteries and of their solution (on the Freudian level, this is even more obvious. Lesik has shown this type of curiosity from the age of three).

It's a very good idea for you to divide your studies into two kinds – natural-scientific and artistic. This helps to prevent the drying-up of one's interest (in this connection, I didn't assess Dima's type of character correctly in my time, so that I partly destroyed his interest in study).

Let Tanya tell you about my 'scrawl phenomenon' – a good example of sublimation through transformation of thought-patterns. Briefly, it goes like this. A child draws scrawls, which have no meaning. An adult 'recognizes' something in the scrawls, and tells the child what he sees. The child now begins to draw in a different way – he transforms his scrawls. The new level of meaning influences the scrawls themselves – they gradually (through their acquiring of meaning) change into drawings. In exactly the same way sex gives way to love, a child's unrelated sounds ('mumbles') become speech, emotional cries become songs, music. This is putting it too simply, but it would seem a fruitful idea for a pedagogical theory.

That is why I want to make out a 'plan' for Lesik's investigations, experiments and observations: to deepen the level of meaning in his hobbies. It's a really bad thing in child development for inclination and comprehension to become fixed, and never to reach the stage of sublimation.

I don't know if I've managed to explain all this clearly enough. I'm feeling very sleepy, under the influence of the drugs.

The episode at the zoo also pleased me. If he (Lesik) succeeds in combining scientific interest in animal life with an ethical sympathy for every living creature, with an aesthetic humanisation of nature as a whole, a spiritual poetic attitude to nature, he will achieve a desirable spiritual harmony within himself.

I'm very glad for Sasha (for Toma too, of course, but I'm a feminist, a supporter of women; I find them more likeable. This is the Ukrainian in me). I'll write to them next time, as I've already managed a great epistolary effort today. And then I'll have to send one reply to their two letters together.

Write to me, when you feel like it.

I love all your letters, especially those in which you develop a theme.

I can't promise to answer. I don't want to write rubbish. And I'm not always in the mood to write anything that isn't rubbish, nor am I always (almost never, in fact) in a proper state to do so.

Well, goodbye for now. Greetings to all newly married couples and all new parents. I don't quite understand about Daniel. Is he T.'s child? Hm – I find it unexpected and pleasant that they should all get on so well together. It's high time that we abandoned these ridiculous moral prejudices, these moral and emotional barriers.

That you find their child wonderful doesn't surprise me. They're all wonderful, though I must confess that from the age of six months they remind me of little frogs, while they look just like lumps of raw flesh when they are younger – most unaesthetic. But this is, of course, a purely male reaction. I adore children from the age of three upwards, when they become more human.

Well, good-bye again.

Tell the newly weds to write again, without relying on my replying. Just like last time – a separate letter from each one of them. But I'll answer them both together.

Your Lyonya

2.9.73

23. *To a Friend*

Greetings, Julia Alexandrovna!

For you, in the Crimea, all days are of course good days.

Here, it's on the whole been very dull weather. I escape from this dullness – inner and outer – in the books that Tanya sends me.

I've just read the 'Gospel of Thomas', which has been translated in *Ancient and Modern*, and under its impact I tried to write to Tanya about the concepts of 'the fairy-tale of life' and the 'taming of life', which I began to evolve after reading Prishvin's 'Root of Life' ('*Zhen-shen*') and 'Water-Drop'. Unfortunately, I couldn't make use of the excerpts I had copied out from these works, and so my attempt to explain these ideas to Tanya was not really a success.

I shall try to tell you about it, briefly.

Have you read 'Root of Life' and 'Water-Drop'? If not, then do read them. They should appeal to you. They express a very subtle poetic psychology, a philosophy of life.

In working out the following tentative theory, I used the works of Prishvin, Schiller, Saint-Exupéry and A. Grin as textual examples of imagery, and, as theoretical material, I used psychoanalysis, child psychology and structural theory.

From child development studies we know of the 'scrawl phenomenon' – I think I once wrote to you about this (but, alas, I can't remember exactly what I then said, so I'll have to repeat myself). At a certain stage of development, a child draws in 'scrawls'. If an adult 'recognizes' some meaning in these, the child begins to try to adapt his scrawls to that new meaning. The meaning transforms the original action – which begins to become drawing in the true sense. The attribution of content to the child's action influences its form; the 'scrawls' are now drawings in 'meaning' as well as in form.

The child begins from a 'scrawl' in all things (the same happens on the phylogenetic level). In the same way we could talk of scrawls in art, in love, and so on, all of which are constantly being attributed with new meaning and are developed, sublimated and humanized through this process.

Before, I simplified the positive function of myth in development, comparing it to opium (with a narcotic function both negatively – in the sense of an addictive drug – and positively – in the sense of relieving pain). But in actual fact the myth is not only a distorted reflection of factually based reality, nor does it only help us to bear with that reality; it also creates circumstances under which reality is transformed, thus brought closer to the myth. (You understand what I mean by these circumstances?)

The myth, or fairy-tale, so becomes a creative force. By 'myth' I mean a concept wider than that of the purely religious – I mean, especially, the poetization of reality.

A. Grin's 'Scarlet Sails' is just such an example, a story which depicts how a fairy-tale is enacted in real life. I have always understood the stories of Grin (and such works as 'The Basket of Fir Cones' by Paustovsky*) as expressing the merging of the fairy-tale with life. It is this sort of fairy-tale which through itself transforms life, giving it new meaning, that I call the fairy-tale of life.

There is an episode in *The Forsyte Saga* where a married couple relate each other's life stories. Grin uses a very similar device in 'The Voice and the Eye'.

The myth of life is not to be equated only with love, although it is usually more clearly reflected in that sphere than anywhere else in life, which is why the majority of artistic works are dedicated to it. Tsiolkovsky† expresses this fairy-tale aspect of life in his notion of going beyond the 'Cradle'. Often, the myth of life is represented – concentrated and crystallized (as in Stendhal's

---

* K. Paustovsky (1893–1968), prominent Soviet writer.

† K. E. Tsiolkovsky (1857–1935), pioneer in rocketry and science-fiction writer. Tr.

De l'Amour) – in the form of an image (or emblem). This gives rise to the image of the 'Scarlet Sails', of Christ, of the girl-deer or root of life – Phatselia in Prishvin's story, the Rose in the case of 'The Little Prince'.

Now I put together these two – the 'scrawl' and the myth. And the fairy-tale of life is born. It emerges as a sublimation of the 'scrawl', when the scrawl takes on a new meaning which it originally lacked – the fairy-tale. The fairy-tale becomes a magnet, drawing to itself the 'scrawl's evolution. The beast in 'The Scarlet Flower' turns into a handsome prince, the frog into a princess, the deer in Prishvin's story into yet another princess.

In the end, all culture is the gradual evolution of the human being from the Darwinian–Freudian beast.

The concept of 'taming' is inherently linked with the fairy-tale of life. The more man develops an individual self, the more terrible the problem of absolute loneliness becomes for each individual – loneliness in the midst of nature and among other people. All human culture (and here I include civilisation) is basically directed towards the solution of this problem, the problem of man reaching out beyond the bounds of his own self, trying to relate to the Other, and to Nature. This relationship materialises in two guises – possession and taming.

Possession alienates man from his background (environment), depriving him of its inherent value and independence. In 'The Frog-Princess' this is pictured in the encroachment on the frog's territory – the burning of its skin; in 'Root of Life', it is in the writer's craving to capture the deer; in *The Forsyte Saga* in Fleur's possessiveness towards John (I can't remember exactly the two other characters – Fleur's father and his wife).

As for the process of 'taming', I am not able to describe it so clearly. Prishvin defines it well, in the deer and Phatselia. It also appears in 'The Little Prince' (The Fox and the Rose). 'Taming' is the fairy-tale – as opposed to the ham-fisted – handling of anything. 'Taming' is piercing through the mystery of the 'Other', respecting that mystery and the Other's inherent value, his individuality. In the process of 'taming', the Rose takes on a form different to that of all other roses. (This is its fairy-tale guise. How, in reality, can the Prince's Rose be any better than a thousand other roses he might see in any hot-house? The magic is in the individual choice – the frog's choice in the fairy-tale, the choice of the deer in Prishvin's story.) The object (of one's choice) gains a value of its own (not as one of many, but treasured because of its originality which, in its inherent characteristics, its uniqueness, identifies with the 'I' making the choice).

The essential point here is that the Other should become a (distinct) 'You' for the 'I' (in the case of possession it is seen as 'not-I').

For every act of possession, the identical words can apply: 'Cain, Cain, where is thy brother Abel? What hast thou done to thy brother?'

These words 'done to' differentiate possession from 'taming'. You can only 'do something to' something alien, unequal in value, usable and lower in status. In the process of 'taming', the 'I', Nature, and the Other are all equal; they may only talk to each other; they don't 'do' anything to each other.

I've explained this better to you than I did to Tanya. Write to me about people, about books.

Yours,
Lyonya

24. *To his Wife*

My darling,

I'm expecting a visit from you today. I've received your 31st letter.

I've been subjected to some changes – I've been transferred to the new block – No. 9. So when you write you'll have to add 'RB-9' on the address.

I find it more difficult to write letters now. I had the notion of writing down my ideas on the constructive-building game. But I just can't do it. Look through those games again, from the stand-point of objectivization–disobjectivization and the origin of the game. The game develops towards a rational plan and a rational construction from objectivized notions.

I've had some delightful letters from Lesik. Write to me more, my darling – from now on your letters will be of even greater help and support to me.

Lesik, write and tell me what you see through your microscope.

Dima! I'm not reading *Technology for the Young* any more, so you can send me extracts from that as well. I'm reading *Science and Life* and the *Literary Gazette*. As from the New Year, I'll be subscribing to *Novy Mir** for six months.

Your Lyonya

22.10.73

---

* Well-known literary journal, meaning 'New World'. *Tr.*

PART TWO

DIAGNOSIS
AND TREATMENT

THE DIAGNOSIS: MEDICAL AND LEGAL ASPECTS

L. I. Plyushch, a mathematician by profession and a member of the Initiative Group for the Defence of Human Rights in the USSR, was arrested in the town of Kiev on 15 January 1972 on charges of anti-Soviet activity.

Until 29 April 1972, he was held in a Kiev investigation prison of the Ukrainian KGB. He was interrogated, but chose to remain silent.

After the interrogation period he was transferred to Moscow, to the investigation wing of the Lefortovo prison. Meanwhile, in Kiev the interrogation of witnesses still went on.

In the middle of October 1972 he was taken back to the Kiev investigation prison.

In December 1972 the investigation came to an end. Plyushch's wife was now informed – for the first time – that her husband had been declared mentally ill.

A year after Plyushch was arrested, his trial took place in the Kiev regional court, from 25 to 29 January 1973. The trial was held in closed court, because, according to Judge Dyshel, 'the evidence to be examined by the court is a State secret'.

The court-room was empty. The only persons present were the three members of the court, the prosecutor and the defence lawyer. The accused was not called, nor were any expert witnesses. Plyushch's wife and relatives were not allowed into court.

The decision of the court was that 'L. Plyushch should be sent for compulsory treatment in a special-type hospital'.

For six months, until July 1973, the highest legal institutions of the Ukraine were deciding the type of psychiatric hospital to which Plyushch should be sent (this involved an appeal hearing, a Procurator's appeal, and a session of the Supreme Court of the Ukraine). On 5 July 1973 the Supreme Court of the Ukraine pronounced its final decision: 'Leonid Ivanovich Plyushch is to be sent for compulsory treatment to a special psychiatric hospital, owing to the especially dangerous nature of his anti-Soviet activities'.

In reality, there had been no 'activities'. Plyushch's 'crime' consisted only of the fact that he had signed letters of appeal sent by the Initiative Group to the UN, and had kept *samizdat* material in his home, together with manuscripts of his own philosophical and ethical works.

In sending him for compulsory treatment, the authorities based themselves on the conclusions of two forensic-psychiatric examinations carried out in Moscow.* In fact Plyushch was subjected to three forensic-psychiatric examinations (one in Kiev, two in Moscow), of which *not one* was carried out under in-patient conditions.

The *first psychiatric examination*, in March–April 1972, was carried out by experts from the forensic-psychiatric department of the Kiev regional hospital (Dr. Lifshits, Head of Department, Dr. Vinarskaya and Dr. Kravchuk) in the prison conditions of the KGB investigation prison in Kiev. According to this examination, the subject was 'a psycho-pathological personality', 'behaved somewhat demonstratively, had exaggerated pretensions and mannerisms',† and was erratic.

Procurator Maly, a procurator responsible for supervising the KGB, has stated that 'no such examination took place in the case of L. I. Plyushch', and this was backed up somewhat later by Plyushch's lawyer, Krzhepitsky. However, it is well known to me that the Kiev examination did take place. This can be confirmed by Matilda Solomonovna Chechik, who was a psychiatric expert for twenty years in that hospital and personally saw the report of

---

* I apologise in advance for any inaccuracies in presenting the diagnoses. These are unavoidable in the circumstances of 'strict secrecy' connected with the case. The quotations from the diagnoses are given here on the basis of two different sources.

† A quotation from 'L. Plyushch's medical history' in its Kiev version.

the commission. In September 1973, Matilda Chechik left the Soviet Union for Israel.

The *second psychiatric examination* was carried out by a Commission of experts from the Serbsky Institute under the chairmanship of G. V. Morozov, Director of the Institute and corresponding member of the Academy of Medical Sciences; it was conducted in the investigation wing of the Lefortovo prison, and took the form of a two-hour conversation.

The Commission concluded:

The case evidence, the hand-written manuscripts, and the results of the examination all testify to the fact that L. I. Plyushch is suffering from a psychiatric illness – sluggish schizophrenia. From his youth he has suffered from paranoid disturbance, characterised by reformist ideas, emotional disturbances and a neurotic attitude to his condition. He is a danger to society: he must be considered not answerable for his actions, and should be sent to a special psychiatric hospital for compulsory treatment.*

Comments on the Commission's Report

The 'handwritten manuscripts' confiscated during a search consisted of drafts for future articles on morality and ethics, explorations into the field of social philosophy and psychology of the personality, and notes on literary works.

It is unbelievably difficult, in our conditions, to write honestly on such subjects. A thinking man, a writer, has to avoid keeping his work in his own house if he wishes to avoid it falling into the clutches of the KGB and disappearing into KGB files. Because of these circumstances, someone ignorant of the difficulties involved might find such manuscripts 'strange', or might think they resembled fragments of thoughts begun and never finished, containing as they usually do many omissions and ellipses. These works often contain only comments on some concept or other, with no explanation, and thus can only be deciphered by the author himself; this is, in fact, what he hopes to do at some time

---

* The Conclusions of the second medical Commission, and of the third Commission (quoted below) were read out by Procurator Maly. The quotations were written down from his actual words, for the Moscow version of the present work.

in the future. Naturally, such fragments can, if one so wishes, be interpreted as 'naïve opinions', 'unconnected thought patterns', 'chaotic nonsense', and so on.

The second psychiatric examination did not satisfy the investigators, for some reason, and they demanded a fresh diagnosis. This is how the investigators' demand was argued: 'The report was based on the case evidence and *clinical observation*. No use was made of experimental psychological or biochemical evidence, or of observation of higher nervous activity.'*

A *third psychiatric examination* was ordered, under the chairmanship of A. V. Snezhnevsky, member of the Academy of Medical Sciences. The Commission concluded:

The patient is suffering from a chronic psychiatric disorder, in the form of schizophrenia. The most prominent features of the illness have been its early beginnings and the development of paranoid disturbance involving elements of fantasising and naïve opinions: this has determined his behaviour pattern. Recent symptoms include the appearance of inventive ideas in the field of psychology: he has an *uncritical* attitude to *what he has done*. Constitutes a danger to society; needs treatment in a psychiatric hospital.

His condition has worsened since the first examination took place [i.e. the first one in Moscow] . . . Some disturbance has become apparent in the emotional-volitional sphere (apathy, indifference, passivity); his stable concern with reformism has been evolving into a concern with innovation in the field of psychology; . . . He should be sent for compulsory treatment in a psycho-neurological hospital.†

Apparently this third examination satisfied the investigators, although on this occasion it had consisted entirely of conversations, one of which (the last) was conducted by Academician A. Snezhnevsky: there were no psychological tests or any other kind of medical investigations.

---

* This quotation is taken from the defence lawyer's written appeal to the USSR Supreme Court (quoted here without his consent). The Supreme Court refused to investigate the case any further, as it considered the verdict given by the Supreme Court of the Ukraine sufficiently proved.

† This quotation is taken from the defence lawyer's written appeal to the USSR Supreme Court (quoted without his consent).

Comments

1. At the time of the final examination (in October 1972), Plyushch had already spent many months in a state of complete isolation from the outside world – he knew nothing of what was happening to his family, his children, his friends – and he was very homesick ('apathy', 'indifference').

2. Plyushch adopted the position that he would not contribute either to the investigation or to any court proceedings, as he feels that no one has the right to judge anyone else for his beliefs. He continued to adopt this attitude during the medical examinations.

3. While in the investigation prison Plyushch wrote an article on 'Game Morphology' and also wrote a number of fairy-tales, which he included in letters to his children (these were never received). Unfortunately, it has proved impossible to add this article and the letters to the letters and article by Plyushch which are published in this volume: they have been attached to his: 'Medical History' and are now in Dnepropetrovsk psychiatric prison.

On 15 July 1973 Plyushch was transferred to the special psychiatric hospital in the town of Dnepropetrovsk.

II.2

THERAPEUTIC INSTITUTIONS OF SPECIAL TYPE

All special psychiatric hospitals in the USSR are, according to the law, officially under the direction of the Ministry of the Interior, the MVD, which also supervises all prisons and labour camps (corrective-labour colonies) in the Soviet Union.

Many of the 'special' hospitals are in the buildings of former prisons or on the premises of present-day ones. For example:

– The Special Psychiatric Hospital in Leningrad was a women's prison in pre-revolutionary times.

– The Special Psychiatric Hospital in Oryol (in the same building as the present-day prison) was a prison before the revolution, when it became known to history as 'the Oryol Central'.

– The Special Psychiatric Hospital in Chernyakhovsk (in the Kaliningrad region, formerly Köningsberg) is a former German prison.

– The Special Psychiatric Hospital in Sychevka (Smolensk region) is a former prison or military prison, built in the time of Catherine I: it was a German hard-labour prison during the occupation in the last war.

The heads of psychiatric prisons, the senior doctors, the heads of regime administration, the heads of supply departments, the supervisors* – all are officers of the MVD with military titles; the service staff (orderlies and domestic staff) are convicted criminals serving terms of imprisonment.

The methods of detention, the attitude of the staff, the general conditions of treatment (overcrowded cells with virtually no ventilation, the lack of fresh air, the dirty convict's clothing) all bear witness to the fact that these hospitals are not therapeutic institutions, but places of imprisonment for the mentally ill.

People who have formally been declared ill are classed in the same category as convicted criminals and treated as such. At the same time, people who are just as sick and dangerous as the latter but have committed no crime, are treated in ordinary psychiatric hospitals (such as, for instance, the Kashchenko hospital in Moscow, or Hospital No. 5 in the village of Stolbovaya in the Moscow region). This division is absurd. Sick people are sick people, and they should be treated, not held in prisons.

However, people such as Professor Lunts insist on the necessity for such prisons; he argues that simply to be in a 'special' hospital is, thanks to the almost total isolation, of special benefit for treating schizophrenics in those cases where the latter have committed crimes.†

This is the more inhuman when people whose only 'crime'

---

* Supervisors – persons in charge of the so-called 'patients under surveillance'. Dissenters are included in the latter category.

† I have personally heard Prof. Lunts make such a statement at the trial of N. Gorbanevskaya, when he was called on to answer questions as an expert.

consists of daring to have a 'particular point of view' (i.e. their own point of view) and to defend it are held in such conditions. Precisely because of the inhumanity involved, the practice is . strictly concealed as being a 'State secret'.

II.3

'HERE IT'S TERRIBLE, HERE IT'S SO TERRIBLE'*

The special psychiatric hospital was quite recently established in the town of Dnepropetrovsk, within the confines of the town prison. The white brick wall surrounding it is topped with three rows of barbed wire. A second wall, also with barbed wire on top, is visible behind the outer wall, and behind that is a red-brick building, with a white square block rising in the centre. This is the Dnepropetrovsk psychiatric prison.

Nothing else is visible. No trees are to be seen, because there are none; the box-like stone construction is a small exercise-yard. It was here that Leonid Plyushch, already branded a criminal-lunatic, was brought in July 1973. Here none of the inmates ever has a peaceful moment or can complain of the conditions in which they are forced to live from year to year. To complain is strictly forbidden and who would believe mentally disturbed people who are given to 'elements of fantasising', 'naïve opinions', 'night-mares and delusions'?

The patients are kept in cells containing between twenty and twenty-five people; there are bars on the windows; the cells are badly lit and cold. We have not been able to discover how large the cells are, or the number of windows, or even if sheets are provided for the beds. Neither have we been able to ascertain what and how often the patients eat. They are shaved of all bodily hair, and given dirty underwear and old prison clothing to wear,

* Leonid Plyushch's own words.

the same clothes as the convicted criminals working in the hospital. One hour of exercise per day is allowed.

But is it only this that produces depression, concealed anxiety, and finally simple fear, in both sick and healthy people detained in institutions of this kind?

Why is there some strange, scarcely definable but quite special and unusual quality in their resignation?

Let us turn to the evidence of some witnesses:*

1. *The Story of an Eye-Witness*†
The Special Psychiatric Hospital in the town of Sychevka, in the Smolensk region, directly adjoins a labour camp, from which it is divided only by a wooden fence.

Out of the 600 convicted criminals in the camp, 200 work in the psychiatric prison as orderlies. In addition, many of the camp prisoners are either former patients or former orderlies of the 'hospital'. There is an unavoidable leakage of information from here, in spite of the painstaking surveillance of the guards (for example, orderlies leaving the psychiatric prison for the camp are first stripped naked and searched).

It is thanks to this leakage of information that we have been able to establish the following facts:

The patients are completely in the power of the illiterate, violent orderlies, who use physical force to make them obey. They call all the patients 'loonies' to their faces and behind their backs. One convict, a former orderly, recalled his days there nostalgically:

'It's great working in the loony-bin: there's always someone whose face you can bash in.'

'What do you want to beat people up for?'

'Just for fun. There you are standing in the corridor, and along comes a loony, holding on to the wall. Well, you get bored, don't you? So I just land him one in the snout, and I feel much better.'

---

* Unfortunately, I have no further information on the Dnepropetrovsk Special Psychiatric Hospital, other than that given in this chapter.

† The name of this eye-witness is known to me: he is willing to substantiate his story.

Another orderly (a tall, strong, healthy lad) complained:

'My hands hurt today.'

'How come?'

'I've been beating up one of the loonies.'

A third told this story:

'The doctor says to me, why is the ward so dirty? When he goes out, I just given the first loony I see a poke in the neck and I say – 'Go on, clean the floor this minute and clear it all up, so it'll all shine like a mirror'.

Beatings take place not only for punishment, but just for personal satisfaction.

The patient-prisoners are not allowed tobacco. The orderlies get it for them. The price of tobacco is twenty 'blows' (by hand) or twenty-five 'lashes' with a brass-buckle belt. This is all an accepted system, so that the authorities and the doctors can hardly help knowing about it.

In some rooms one pair of slippers has to be shared between seven or eight patients, so that the patients are forced to stay in bed. The patients cannot perform their natural functions, as the orderlies do not always take them to the lavatory at their first request. The patients themselves do not have the right to go there alone, so they sometimes have to wait for hours.

The psychiatric prison has a library. However, the patients do not have the right to use it. In this way the majority of patients find themselves condemned to weary inactivity or monotonous work such as making nets.

The doctors misuse their injections; they use them not only for medical treatment but also as punishment – e.g. for rude answers from a patient, or following a complaint from an orderly, etc. Besides this, the 'chaining-up' method is widely used: a patient is tied to his bunk, sometimes for days at a time (usually this is done to openly aggressive patients).

There are ten departments in the hospital. (The worst ones are the seventh and the tenth departments.) The patients are of various categories: convicts who became ill while in labour camps (when they are released from the hospital, they are sent back to the labour camp); the cases of simulation and exaggeration –

criminals who have bestial murders on their consciences and prefer a psychiatric hospital to the death penalty or a life sentence in the camps; there are also a number of people imprisoned for religious reasons. Many are sent to Sychevka from Moscow, Leningrad and the Ukraine. There are also people who are held for political reasons (e.g. Yuri Belov and Mikhail Kukobaka).*

2. *Seven Times in Kazan*† *by Yury Iofe*

It was like this:

> I woke in the morning,
> Looked out of the window . . .
> All around – Soviet power.

The Kazan special prison, or special psychiatric hospital, institution UE 148/ST–6, is situated in a bare, lonely spot, behind white brick walls, on the banks of the river Kazanka.

The head of this institution is Dr. A. R. Merdeyev: he wears a military uniform under his white coat.

The visitors' room is a low, dirty-white passage-way with small barred windows. It contains two ornaments: a clock and a portrait of Chekhov, author of 'Ward No. 6'; under the portrait hangs a placard displaying the famous quotation: 'In a human being everything should be beautiful – the face, the clothing, the soul and the mind. . . ."

The clock is inexorable: it beats out every minute of a visit.

That is a description of the exterior. I have not seen the inside. I only know what I have heard about it.

This is what I have discovered:

Ward No. 93, where my daughter‡ was kept, is not large (14 square metres). It has bluish-green walls, the door is of a lighter colour. The door has a feeding-trough in it. Opposite the door is

* See details of their cases in the *Chronicle of Current Events*, Nos. 9, 18, 26 and 27.

† Only those extracts from Iofe's 'Documentary Poetic Sketch No. 5' which are closely relevant to the theme of this chapter are given here.

‡ Olga Iofe, charged under Article 70 of the RSFSR Criminal Code; on 20 June 1970 was sent to Kazan special psychiatric hospital for treatment, on the orders of the Moscow City Court. Olga was then twenty years old. See *Chronicle of Current Events*, No. 15.

a window, through the bars of which the sun is visible; it sets behind the white brick wall, behind the black trees, somewhere beyond the river Kazanka. During the hours of darkness, Ward No. 93 is lit by an unshaded light which cannot be switched off.

There are five to six people in the ward, mostly murderers. I shall name a few of its inhabitants – my daughter's room-mates, and some others she got to know on her walks in the courtyard.

Vera Ivanovna: forty-one years old. Killed her mother with an axe. Considers herself to be Vilya, Queen of England Crosses herself constantly to keep the demons away, as these demons are trying to assault her, the English Queen, from behind. Reptiles are also trying to overpower her. This is why she keeps asking Olga to take the snake off her back.

Anida Hecht: a German by nationality, obviously a deportee. Crippled her father. Convinced that only Russians are being cured, Germans are being crippled. Aggressive, like her namesake, the pike (*Hecht* means a pike in German).

Tatyana Guseva: age unknown (still registered as sentenced under Article 58, in accordance with the Stalinist system) – imprisoned for committing an offence against the State flag. According to prison tradition, she entered the prison as a healthy young girl with thick plaits. Now, after twelve years of treatment, she is shaven-headed and completely reduced to a state of idiocy.

Olga Nozhak: age unknown, Article 58. She has been here for sixteen years. She is an enthusiastic guitar player, hunch-backed from constant guitar-playing. Composes songs, the most popular being 'Arise, prisoner of Kazan' – she sings this to the tune of the 'Internationale'. Besides singing, she shouts slogans.

Lyuba, nicknamed 'Telly', thirty-eight years old, looks about fifty, 1.5 metres waistline. Killed her lover on the seventh day of their happy life together: she had a delusion that he had robbed her of 20 roubles. She trades the products from her parcels with other prisoners (one garlic for 10 kopecks). When she was free, she lived with her father.

Maria Shchekach, no age, an imbecile from birth. Incontinent. In her spare time burrows round in the lavatories, carefully collecting the contents and painstakingly hiding these in the pockets of her dressing-gown. Calls all men 'grandad' and all women 'Masha'.

Khovrya Petrakova, half-paralysed, completely shaved of all bodily hair, a creator of obscene songs, which she sings in a loud voice:

> 'Out of its hole a public louse
> Poked its little head.
> Start f——ing, will you,
> I'm dying of hunger, it said.'

She accompanies the songs by spitting and sometimes by vomiting. The orderlies enthusiastically call for encores. Khovrya also masturbates with sweet-papers.

The other patients in institution UE–148/ST–6 are of the same sort. Onanists, lesbians, nymphomaniacs.

One of them, whose name I don't know, sits bare-bottomed on the snow, and lovingly shoves her finger into that place which an inspired poet called 'the secret, rosy grotto' and which has a much simpler and more resounding name in common speech.

Another came up and passionately kissed my daughter, while she was sitting on the lavatory.

And so on.

Every day there are violent fights – about shower places, about slippers and quilts.

> 'And this does not prevent
> us eating, drinking, smoking,
> dressing, fornicating, undressing
> and so enjoying life.'

And Olya is twenty years old!

A few words about the medical staff:

Olga Ivanovna Volkova: Doctor. She is convinced she can 'see through' everyone. When releasing anyone she says tenderly: 'You'll be coming back some day.'

Rosa: Orderly, a soul-saving provocateur who calls everyone 'my dearest'.

The service personnel are prisoners (sane ones). These happily torment the other, insane prisoners. A certain Slavik was especially notorious for this – he used to beat up women who were tied to their beds. For his zeal this benefactor received all kinds of privileges from the authorities, including glucose drinks, no doubt to keep up his strength.

'The institutional forms of Soviet legal psychiatry give real guarantees that the rights of the mentally ill will be protected' – Dr. Lunts, doctor of medical science, professor. (In *Soviet Legal Psychiatry*, published by *Znanie*, 1970, p. 32.)

On 22–23 August, Plyushch was allowed his first meeting with his wife, a year and a half after his arrest. The meeting took place in accordance with the rules of psychiatric hospitals – at a distance of 2 metres from each other, in the presence of two prison officials.

Soon his first letters began to arrive.

Leonid Ivanovich begged his wife to get him transferred somehow to any other hospital, of the same type (in Oryol, Leningrad, Kazan, it didn't matter which). 'What goes on here is simply not to be compared with anywhere else. The people from Kazan are trying to get back to Kazan.'*

On the day of their meeting, 22 August, the 'patient' was given haloperidol for the first time. Why he should be given haloperidol, no one would explain.

'What dose?'

'The individual dose.'

'Your husband is seriously ill,' added Dr. E. P. Kamenetskaya,† 'we shall be treating him for a long time with various drugs: first haloperidol, then we'll start him on something else.'

Leonid Plyushch has asked people not to send him literary works. Creative literature arouses the kind of emotions that make it impossible to ignore one's surroundings, and therefore it cannot

---

* These are patients who have been transferred from the Special Psychiatric Hospital in Kazan to the Dnepropetrovsk Special Psychiatric Hospital.

† Ella Petrovna Kamenetskaya (Head of the 12th Department at Dnepropetrovsk Special Psychiatric Hospital; she was Plyushch's first doctor there); she refused to give us her name, not even her first name – 'That's not our custom here.' We got to know it later, but not from her.

be read. He wants to try to continue his scientific research: science always absorbed him completely. The investigation prison now seems to him like paradise: at least there he could read; there he wrote 'Game Morphology'.

Leonid Plyushch has not abandoned his convictions or changed his point of view. He does not consider himself ill and has therefore refused to accept the pension he was offered, as an invalid suffering from a psychiatric disorder.

II.4

WARD NO. 9

On Friday, 19 October, L. Plyushch's wife, Tatyana Ilyinichna Zhitnikova,* arrived in Dnepropetrovsk for a regular visit to her husband; she took her son Dima with her.

She was not allowed to meet her husband: 'L. Plyushch has been transferred to another ward. As the patient in the next bed to him has fallen ill with a very infectious complaint, your husband is now in quarantine. You could try coming again on Monday; perhaps the situation will be clearer by then and you will be able to see your husband.'

The three days which Tatyana Zhitnikova and her son had to spend in Dnepropetrovsk were distressing for her. She was tormented by uncertainty. Why had her husband been transferred to another department? Was it better for him there, or worse? Would she see him this time or would she have to return to Kiev, without seeing him?

Each journey to Dnepropetrovsk required money, and they hardly had any. Tatyana Zhitnikova was supporting her two children and Leonid Ivanovich himself on her salary: she was trying to send Leonid more useful foods, if only these would be accepted.

* In the USSR it is quite usual for a wife to retain her own surname after marriage. *Tr.*

This time Tatyana Ilyinichna had brought their son with her, whom his father inquired about in almost every letter – this had made the journey twice as expensive.

However, that was not the most important thing. Leonid Ivanovich himself mattered most; he always waited so eagerly for the times when she visited him! At present he lived only for these meetings with her. His science studies helped him to cut himself off from his surroundings, to bury himself in his own thoughts, to avoid looking around him . . . and to make time pass more quickly, until their next meeting.

Her disquiet was increasing steadily. Tatyana Ilyinichna was all the more worried because she had noticed, on the first day when they arrived in Dnepropetrovsk, that she and her son were being constantly followed by KGB agents. Why was this? Perhaps something had happened to her husband? In addition, this surveillance made things very difficult for her: how was she to avoid bringing trouble on those who had let her and her son stay with them for these three to four days?

Monday came. Permission was given for the visit; even her son was allowed to be present.*

When Leonid Ivanovich was brought into the visiting room, he was unrecognizable. His eyes showed that he was depressed and in pain, he spoke with difficulty, in disconnected phrases, often throwing himself against the back of the chair as if in need of support. It was obvious how hard he was trying to control himself; he tried to carry on a conversation, to answer questions, at times with his eyes closed. But his inner strength was exhausted, completely at an end. Leonid Ivanovich began to find it difficult to breathe, he unbuttoned his shirt with fingers that would not obey him; he began to have convulsions, his face was distorted by twitches, he could no longer control the movements of his arms and legs. He would pull himself upright, shuddering, his whole body tense, and then he would feebly collapse again across the table. It was noticeable that he was losing his sense of hearing at times. But he persevered – before him stood his wife and his son, who was completely disheartened by what he saw – he tried to

* Up till then she had always been told 'It's now allowed'.

speak, twitching and swallowing saliva. Convulsions seized his throat, and affected his speech. Leonid Ivanovich could not bear it and himself asked for the visit to be ended, ten minutes early. He was taken away.

According to rumour, Ward No. 9, for the 'worst cases', is an unbearable place. It has become known to us that there are twenty-six people in this ward, among them many aggressive ('violent') patients. All the patients are shut up in the ward-cell without being able to go out. They are led out only once a day, for an hour's walk, and for visits to the lavatory.

The new doctor in charge of Leonid Plyushch's treatment, Lidiya Alekseyevna,* gives the impression of being a cruel, unfeeling person. In a conversation with Tatyana Zhitnikova, she said that she had not yet been able to acquaint herself with the 'patient's' case, so that she could not tell her very much about him.

'I have not yet noticed any signs of "philosophical intoxication" in him. . . . However, the patient has showed a tendency to "mathematization of psychology and medicine". I am a doctor and I am aware that mathematics has nothing to do with medicine.'

When asked what kind of drugs Leonid Ivanovich was being given (he was being given tablets of some sort three times a day), the doctor declined to give an answer:

'Why should you know that? We give him what he needs.'

During their meeting, Plyushch had told his wife that he was now unable even to write her letters. He had tried, had managed to write half a page only, and had not sent it. In answer to his wife's insistent pleas, he promised to go on sending letters, even if they only consisted of one line.

Soon it became known that after the visit, Plyushch had taken a turn for the worse: he was racked by continuous convulsions; he kept jumping up and lying down again, moving his arms, legs and whole body around – nothing helped. He did not sleep all night.

Two weeks passed. During this time his wife received only one short letter from her husband.

* She refused to give her surname (later found to be Chasovskikh). *Tr.*

It was now time for her next visit, on 6 November 1973. Again she was worried and waited anxiously fearing that this time they would not see each other, perhaps because of her husband's physical condition.

They did see each other. In addition, Plyushch's physical condition had improved: there were no spasms or convulsions, he managed to hold out until the end of the visit. The explanation was simple – his dose of drugs had been decreased to 30 mg. (the amount given earlier is unknown). The drug was administered in drops. He was obviously not being given a corrective drug; at least, he was being given nothing except these drops – no other drops or powders, or tablets such as cyclodol.

On this occasion their conversation was interrupted by the comments of a girl in white overalls, who was continuously present at visits.

'He might get confused, and not be able to tell you what he means, and you might misunderstand.'

Plyushch was in a state of continual drowsiness; he could not read, but had written a letter, with some difficulty, on the day before. (The previous Sunday, he had missed the time allotted for writing letters as he had been unable to write anything.) He now asked that scientific books should not be sent to him, for the time being: not only could he not read, he was unable even to think properly.

His state was generally apathetic. He listened more than he spoke. His wife felt that he found it difficult to speak; at first he even hiccuped when speaking. He hardly asked about anything. He was losing the lively interest he had always felt in everyone and everything. Everything seemed hopeless and meaningless to him. Nobody and nothing could be of any help.*

The only requests he made to his wife were:

(1) 'Take care of yourself, don't let anything happen to you.'

(2) 'I realize this is futile, but could you ask, all the same, that

* An International Seminar on Schizophrenia had just been held in the USSR (8–12 October), and this had given rise to publicity for Soviet psychiatric abuse as regards Plyushch and other dissenters.

I be transferred back to Department No. 12 [see previous section]. There it was at least possible, for example, to wash out one's own underwear; here it is not allowed.' (Perhaps it was because of this that he asked not to be given soap or tobacco. He did not explain why.)

He complained that his teeth (or gums) were hurting, and for this reason asked that nothing should be given to him that was difficult to eat, such as smoked sausage, biscuits, carrots or radishes.

He asked everyone to forgive him for not replying to their letters, and yet asking them to write to him. He added: 'Letters are given to me only so that I can read them, and afterwards they are taken away. In this way I was also briefly shown photographs of my family, wife and children.'

At this point, the doctor in charge of his treatment entered the visiting room and greeted all those present on the occasion of the Great October anniversary.* Instead of giving the usual answering greeting, Tatyana Zhitnikova asked a question:

'I'm interested in your diagnosis of my husband, L. I. Plyushch. Why is he being given haloperidol? Is he being given a corrective drug or not?'

'What corrective drug? And why do you want to know?'

'I know he is being given haloperidol. This explains the attack my husband had, which I witnessed on my last visit.'

'But has Leonid Ivanovich been complaining? After all, we have a very good relationship with him. Isn't that true, Leonid Ivanovich?'

Leonid Ivanovich did not answer. Only a spark of malevolence, so foreign to his character, appeared in his glance for a moment, but was quickly suppressed by an effort of will.

'As regards your question,' said the doctor, turning to Tatyana Zhitnikova, 'I shall tell you nothing: neither my diagnosis, nor the drugs we use to cure.'

Leonid Ivanovich was led away. The visit was over. But his wife's troubles were not over: she felt obliged to turn to the hospital authorities for an explanation. She was received by

* The anniversary of the October 1917 Bolshevik Revolution (7 November).

Valentina Yakovlevna Katkova,* the deputy head of the medical department of Dnepropetrovsk Special Psychiatric Hospital.

V. Y. Katkova heard out what Tatyana Zhitnikova had to say, and her requests – (1) that Plyushch should be transferred back to Department No. 12, and (2) that he should be allowed to keep just a few of the letters and photographs sent to him by members of his family.

In answer to the first request, V. Katkova began to speak in a benevolent tone about their hospital – how good it was, how many people wanted to be admitted to it.

'They don't really know,' she remarked in passing, 'what people are here *for*, but they know we *cure* them. We're the Moscow school.'

'Snezhnevsky's school?'†

'Yes . . .' proudly . . . 'Snezhnevsky. Don't imagine that we experiment,‡ we treat everyone strictly according to established methods. Everyone is satisfied with our results; professors come to visit us.'

After discoursing in this manner, she turned to answering the requests:

'A transfer to his former department will be impossible, as that was a somatic department – it's for people suffering not only from nervous disorders, but also from tuberculosis, ulcers and liver diseases. We often transfer the patients. And in any case, there's no room there at the moment; there's nowhere to put even an extra bed.'

'Well, what about the letters and photographs?'

'Letters – you know, when a lot of them pile up, they could become infested with cockroaches. We don't have cockroaches, of course, but anything could happen. But a photo – well all right, it's a modest request [*sic*!] – and a few letters, I'll try to arrange it; I think it might be possible to leave him a few.'

---

* We found her surname on a list posted in the hall, which contained the names of all members of the staff.

† See page viii.

‡ What was this? The subconscious at work?

PART THREE

III.1

LEONID PLYUSHCH THROUGH THE EYES OF HIS FRIENDS

(i) A mathematician, also engaged in the study of biology and psychology, a man of great intellectual ability and wide intellectual and cultural interests – has been declared mentally ill and confined to a special psychiatric hospital.

People like L. Plyushch are not considered good material for trials, they are dangerous: they inspire apprehension in those investigating their case, because of their marvellous steadfastness, their moral irreproachability, and they therefore prefer to declare them mentally ill.

In the years preceding his arrest, Leonid Plyushch wrote a number of works, deeply thought out and varied in subject-matter. He wrote of man's spiritual nature in the modern world, of moral and historical progress. He was searching for a definition of that most important concept – the meaning of life. This was why he examined such interesting, important and varied themes in his work as Christianity and the fight against God in the poetry of Shevchenko; Tolstoy and Tolstoyan ideas in the epoch of scientific revolution; Dostoyevsky and Marx; the third-rate works of certain Soviet writers as examples of social-pathological anxiety symptoms.

His works have now been taken away, confiscated, perhaps destroyed. The wonderful human brain that created them is now consciously feeling and observing the destruction of its own ability to think and create.

T. Velikanova
S. Kovalov
G. Podyapolsky
T. Khodorovich

(ii) One common sorrow unites us all, people of various opinions, in writing these lines. It is difficult to describe the impression made on us, the close friends of Leonid Ivanovich Plyushch, by the official announcement that according to a medical examination carried out in the Serbsky Institute, in Moscow, he had been declared mentally ill and was now in a special mental hospital.

The absurdity of what had happened was so obvious, and Leonid Ivanovich's personality was so strongly linked, in our minds, with that mental health which had been a source of support for so many others who needed it, that we did not yet realize the extent of the tragedy.

He is a Marxist by conviction, a scientist by ability and choice; he was, at the age of thirty-three, at the height of his creative powers. His main interests were cybernetics, mathematics, the theory of games, social psychology, the study of culture.

The main characteristic of his personality was a continuous moral quest.

Friendship with Plyushch always seemed to come about in an imperceptible, easy way. People who varied greatly in their views found it easy to get on with him.

In the course of many years we have had the opportunity of seeing something of Plyushch's family life. He has a wife and two children. In his house an atmosphere of moral security and simple human happiness reigned. Only now, when we see how that has been destroyed, do we understand how necessary the whole spirit and structure of that family was to many of us as a spiritual support.

There are no new tragedies in life. Everything in this world has already happened before. Yet, all the same, the thought that somewhere nearby in our country – in Dnepropetrovsk or in Kazan – willing or unwilling executioners are deliberately using the achievements of science in order to destroy the soul of a living human being, a wonderful man – such a thought makes one's blood run cold.

Only emigration abroad can save L. I. Plyushch. We realise quite clearly that otherwise only destruction awaits him. Neither he himself, nor his relatives, can have any control over the drugs

which are being injected into his organism.
His Friends

I met Plyushch in May 1972. I had already undergone – and he was about to undergo – a legal-psychiatric examination. Our happiness – as two Marxists, meeting each other – did not last long: a few hours later we were separated.*

Leonid's Marxism was deeply thought out, and was not merely an outer garment, the wearing of which was to be a sign for everyone to accept you and behave well towards you. Neither was he a fanatic with extreme views. Leonid's thinking was precise, well reasoned and to the point. He would consider a question, dispute it, listen, make ironic comments, agree, reject some statement he had made. He was a joy to listen to, because of his self-possession, his decisiveness, his conviction.

L. Plyushch was a man in full mental health, so that I was quite astounded to hear the news that he had been declared insane. This is a mistake which must be corrected. What is even more horrifying is the fact that he is being treated forcibly, without his consent or that of his wife. This is a crime which must be stopped.

Vaclav Sevruk†

I met Leonid Plyushch on a number of occasions, in 1970–1, among small groups of people. He attracts people to him almost immediately, through a special inner fascination. He is a modest man, not affected in any way; he does not 'put himself forward', and carefully listens to other people; he spoke very little himself, softly, naturally, to the point; he made wonderfully appropriate and wise remarks and rejoinders; his questions were the same. . . . One of my friends told me that Leonid Plyushch was a Marxist. I was very surprised – could such a reasonable, sensitive and undoubtedly honest man be a Marxist? Somehow, when we were

---

* I remember that Plyushch had had a meal in the Serbsky Institute canteen, and then been taken back again to Lefortovo prison. His examination was not carried out at the Institute.

† On Sevruk (who emigrated in 1974 to the USA) see the *Chronicle of Current Events*, Nos. 15, 22, 24, 26, Amnesty International Publications, London.

saying goodbye to him in the passage, I expressed my disbelief on this subject and asked him to 'convince' me. He smiled and replied that he had no wish or desire to force his opinions on others. We had a short conversation on the articles of G. Pomerants* on the study of culture, and I promised to get some for him.

In talking to Leonid Plyushch, you feel yourself at ease, free to say what you like. Unlike some other learned intellectuals, who know their own worth, you feel in him no contempt for others, no sense of superiority, no élitist exclusiveness, and absolutely no dishonesty. After my first meeting with Plyushch I asked many of his friends about him, as they knew him better than I did, and had known him for a longer period.

'Lyonya' – this name has a special sort of sound, when spoken by those who know Leonid Plyushch: people speak of him with amazing warmth, respect and delight!

One of my close friends (a university student of philosophy, greatly interested in literature and philosophy) who at one time was a constant visitor in Leonid Plyushch's home (at the end of the 1960s), often recalled his arguments with Plyushch, which sometimes lasted until after midnight. Leonid Plyushch was a very interesting and indefatigable disputer, who listened very respectfully and attentively to his opponent and quietly argued his point, with excellent knowledge of his subject; he considered argument one of the means of searching for truth.

Leonid Plyushch's company was never boring: everything he did, he did with enjoyment, with a kind of flame. 'Lyonya has a limp [from the tuberculosis of the bone he suffered in childhood], but he walks very fast. I went for a ramble with him along the steep banks of the Dnieper, and I couldn't keep up with him,' said L. (herself an enthusiastic rambler, who liked climbing in picturesque, steep places), a guest at Plyushch's house. . . .

I feel that when people talk about Leonid Plyushch, they become more attractive, better. . . .

I hoped that I would be able to meet and talk to Leonid

* *Grigory Pomerants*, a philosopher and historian specialising in oriental studies, who lives in Moscow and publishes essays in *samizdat*.

Plyushch again. . . . I obtained the articles by G. Pomerants that had interested him, although somewhat later, and wanted to give them to him . . . and then I heard that Leonid Plyushch had been arrested.

During Leonid Plyushch's trial, I got to know his wife Tatyana Ilyinichna Zhitnikova – Tanya. Leonid Plyushch and his wife are a rare case (very rare) of people really finding a partner for life. She is a woman with a wonderful inner warmth and goodness, tolerant, sensitive in relation to other people . . . with unusual inner powers of endurance. Like Leonid Plyushch himself, she is wonderfully healthy in mind and spirit, with great spiritual beauty. . . . The Soviet regime has subjected her to inhumanly cruel, savage treatment.

Of course, Leonid Plyushch is in perfect mental health. But he is not merely a mentally healthy man, he is a man with a wonderful inner poise, a marvellous person!

However, I cannot regard the arrest of Leonid Plyushch, nor his certification as mentally ill or insane, nor his transfer to a special psychiatric hospital (a psychiatric prison) for compulsory treatment, nor his treatment in that 'hospital', as a 'mistake' on the part of the Soviet authorities.

In this respect Dmitri Nelidov* was right when he said in his article: 'Prison torture-chambers were shown to be insufficient, and so someone thought up the Himmler-like idea of imprisonment in a psychiatric hospital.'

This is not merely a 'change in the form of punitive measures', it is a revolutionary leap: the emphasis of punishment is changed from its length to its quality. . . . Health is defined as acceptance of rules previously laid down, of two-faced laws, of the "culture of social adaptation". . . . When double-thinking is the rule, it produces its own concept of the normal man, and begins to measure human worth and wholeness according to that concept. The whole meaning of the "Democratic movement's" political protest was contained in the different norm of human health which it demonstrated, a norm which was found to be insufferable by a society infected by a spiritual disease of epileptic proportions'

* Pseudonym of a *samizdat* author. *Tr.*

('Ideocratic consciousness and the personality', *Samizdat*, September 1973).

*M. N. Landa**

III.2

'THEY THREATENED THAT ANYONE WHO DARED TO REVEAL THE TRUTH TO THE PEOPLE WOULD RECEIVE A TERRIBLE PUNISHMENT'†

The forces of law and order have been trying, and continue to try, to persuade L. Plyushch's wife of something which she cannot admit to be true for as long as she considers herself a human being. They try to persuade her that her husband is suffering from a 'severe mental illness', that he is a 'particular danger to society'.

She has expressed her own attitude to this charge more than once, in a number of letters, statements, appeals and petitions to every possible department of the KGB, the Law Courts, the Procuracy, to both local and all-Soviet authorities. However difficult she must have found it, she even forced herself to write a letter to Academician A. V. Snezhnevsky.

Leonid Ivanovich Plyushch possesses a great quality: he never submits his power of reasoning to anyone else. In all his thoughts, words and deeds, he is motivated only by moral considerations and by his own conscience, and not by self-interested careerism.

Why, for what purpose, did you find it necessary to break, trample underfoot and spiritually destroy my husband? What high ideals inspired you to do this? Surely not the 73 roubles of legal expenses,‡

* Malva Landa is a Moscow geologist. *Tr.*

† 'Extracts from underground Populist publications: 1873–75'; published by 'Nauka', Leningrad 1970. The Populist movement was an attempt by revolutionary intellectuals to bring political enlightenment to the peasants. Its philosophical ideas greatly influenced later generations. *Tr.*

‡ A bill for legal expenses had been addressed to T. I. Zhitnikova, Plyushch's wife; it was dated 24 August 1973, had been issued by the People's Court in the Kiev Lenin region, and was signed 'Lysenko'.

demanded from Plyushch, which also included the fees for your medical examination? Where did you get such an accommodating conscience, where did you acquire the moral right to condemn a healthy man to a life of complete isolation in the company of mentally sick people, where he has no way of defending himself and is completely at the mercy of people who are not subject to any external control?

This is worse than prison, worse than hard labour, worse than murder. How could you have dared to do this, when you have sworn the Hippocratic oath? Does your conscience not bother you? Were you not afraid you would choke on the sorrowful tears of Plyushch's children?

She received no answer to this letter, but merely a notification from the post office that it had been delivered.

In a state of great distress, Tatyana Zhitnikova appealed again to the medical conscience, this time in the person of Dr. Timakov, President of the Academy of Medical Sciences:

Forgive me for troubling you. Please help me! It's impossible to believe all this has really taken place – we are, after all, living among fellow human beings. Help me!

However, not only did the President of the AMS fail to offer any help whatever but, like Academician A. V. Snezhnevsky, he did not even reply to the letter.

But perhaps the legal authorities would behave differently?

In her statement to the Supreme Court of the Ukrainian SSR T. I. Zhitnikova wrote (in part):

The whole conduct of the investigation and trial was more reminiscent of a lynching than a court of justice.

I appeal to the Supreme Court of the Ukrainian SSR and request that the infringements of the law which were permitted in the case of my husband, Leonid Ivanovich Plyushch, be put right by an appeal court.

A written statement was also addressed to the Chairman of the Supreme Court of the Ukrainian SSR by friends of L. I. Plyushch:

We do not know on what the psychiatric examiners based their conclusions, but as people who have known L. I. Plyushch and his family well for a number of years, we take upon ourselves the full responsibility of declaring that L. I. Plyushch is a completely normal healthy person, and we request that a new, open psychiatric examination be carried out, and that the commission of experts should include two psychiatrists nominated by Plyushch's relatives.

We realize that there can be judicial mistakes in any court case. However, no punishment, even an unjust one, would have so astounded everyone who knew L. I. Plyushch, as the court decision to commit him, for an unspecified period, to a special psychiatric hospital for compulsory treatment.

In this case we are not speaking of the usual kind of legal error, but of a much more terrifying kind of error.

We are now speaking of the forcible detention of a healthy man in an institution for the mentally ill, of the introduction into his organism of powerful drugs, intended for the treatment of seriously ill persons; we are speaking of possible menticide, i.e. the murder of a human personality.

It is hard to imagine a human being whose conscience could calmly bear the weight of having made such an error.

A. I. Plyushch, Leonid Plyushch's sister, sent a petition to the Procurator's Office of the Ukrainian SSR, calling for a review of her brother's case:

Neither my mother nor I myself have ever noticed anything strange in my brother's behaviour. He always had many friends, who are very fond of my brother because of his friendly disposition and his tolerance towards other people and their mistakes.

At school, he was always one of the top pupils; he was always ready to help his schoolmates at mathematics; he took part in mathematics competitions and in organizing after-school activities. I write this according to what my mother and his school friends have told me. He received a silver medal on graduating from school.

I consider the days I spent in my brother's company the best days of my life. He was not only good at talking about science and literature in an interesting way, but he also listened carefully to the person he was talking to – and he was always ready to help anyone, if the need arose. This was why he was loved by his relations and friends'

All this brought no results. But let us look at one more appeal written by Plyushch's wife:

Nikolai Viktorovich!
Leonid Ilyich!
Aleksei Nikolayevich!*

I have made every effort to keep the case of L. I. Plyushch within the confines of the law: I have appealed in person and in writing – in

* Addressed to N. Podgorny, L. Brezhnev and A. Kosygin. In Russian, the use of only the name and patronymic at the beginning of a letter is a mark of respect. *Tr.*

statements, petitions and protests – to all possible authorities, including the USSR Procurator's Office and the USSR Supreme Soviet. But this has achieved nothing. I was deprived of every possibility of over-turning the biased charges made at the investigation. I was not per-mitted to nominate a psychiatrist known to me as my representative on the psychiatric examination boards. I was not informed of the times when these examinations took place, nor was I given the opportunity of choosing a lawyer during the investigation, although Plyushch has a right to this. I was not permitted to be present at my husband's trial. I have still not been given a copy of the verdict or even of extracts from it. I have been threatened on two occasions with repressive measures, at militia headquarters (to my indignation, I was cynically informed 'You can complain all you want – your complaints will all be dealt with by us, in any case'). I have not been allowed a single meeting with my husband (16 months have already gone by since his arrest). I have even been forbidden to write to him. . . .

Surely, life in our society is now based on more humane and democratic principles than in the days before the XX Congress of the Party. And I do not believe that what happened to my family is a necessity of state. I think that this injustice is attributable to certain individuals, who have a wrong idea of professional ethics!

Help us, or this wholly heartless, completely inhuman act will really take place – a healthy man will be shut up in a special mental hospital. This fate, equivalent to the horrors of hell, is threatening my husband, myself and our children, in our own country, in the middle of the twentieth century.

One's situation becomes hopeless not when there is no help from anyone but when one no longer wants to ask for help. But it cannot be true that nothing in the world is considered sacred any longer.

It became clear that this was to have no results. And besides this, what else is there to be said? The most eloquent and complete answer to that question is contained, in my opinion, in the following extracts from a certain document, and in everything that followed its appearance.

These are the extracts from the document:

Official Search Report

Town: Kiev   28 August 1973

Sidorenko, Procuracy Investigator of the Darnitsky district of Kiev, carried out a search at Apartment No. 36, Block No. 33 in the Street of Enthusiasts, which apartment belongs to citizen T. I. Zhitnikova, with the aim of finding and confiscating material of a libellous nature. During the search the following objects were discovered and confiscated:

One copy of a letter, typed out, beginning with the words 'Andrey Vladimirovich' and ending with the words 'If my letter does not reach you, I shall try to bring it to your notice in some other way' (3 pages).

One copy of a letter, typed out, beginning with the words 'Respected Comrade Timakov' and ending with the words 'With respect, 26.2.73' (1 page).

A statement by citizen T. I. Zhitnikova to the Supreme Court of the Ukrainian SSR (a copy) (4 typed pages), dated 14 February 1973.

A letter (4 typed pages), beginning with the words 'Nikolai Viktorovich, Leonid Ilyich, Aleksey Nikolayevich!' and ending with the words: 'As I have received no reply, not even a notification that my letter has been delivered to those it was addressed to, I am sending this letter a second time'; dated 7 July 1973. Zhitnikova had five more identical copies of this letter.

A statement addressed to the Chairman of the Supreme Court of the Ukrainian SSR, from S. E. Borshchevsky, A. A. Verkhman, V. E. Yuvchenko, A. D. Feldman, typed out (1 copy), 2 pages, dated March 1973.

A notification (1 page) of the delivery of a letter through the post to Timakov, President of the Academy of Medical Sciences.

A notification of the delivery of a letter through the post to citizen A. V. Snezhnevsky.

The above-mentioned objects were found in a file in a drawer of the writing-table, in Room No. 1 of Zhitnikova's flat.

This means that someone found it necessary to try to frighten Plyushch's wife and make her deny that her husband was a healthy man, as her attempts to defend him were turned against her and called 'libels'.

How can we avoid quoting from the fairy-tale at this point: 'In order that the common people should not disturb the Tsar with complaints about their bitter life, and should not try to bother him with their troubles and needs, the Tsar has numerous guards everywhere, who are supported by our own money.'

On 18 October 1973, T. I. Zhitnikova was taken from her place of work by Investigator Kondratenko of the Town Procurator's Office to the Darnitsky district procurator's department, in Kiev, for a 'talk'. The 'talk' – as Investigator Kondratenko informed her, this exists as a legal category, and is conducted without any record being made – had three main points:

(i) *Zhitnikova's refusal to give evidence in the case of V. A. Nekipelov.** Investigator Kondratenko inquired whether T. I. Zhitnikova had not changed her mind about refusing to give evidence at the trial of V. A. Nekipelov, who had been arrested in Vladimir. The point was that, by law, the Vladimir Procurator's Office had the right to prosecute her on a criminal charge for refusing to give evidence. Zhitnikova replied that she maintained her former intention – she would not give evidence in the case of V. A. Nekipelov – and that she had officially stated this when being interrogated in connection with the case.

'What are your motives for refusing?'

'I'm tired of associating with the representatives of justice; I don't want any further contact with them.'

(ii) *Her links with Zionism*

'What are your connections with Zionism?'

T. I. Zhitnikova did not answer, waiting for some further elucidation of the question.

Investigator Kondratenko took from an envelope a photocopy of the statement made by friends of Plyushch to the Supreme Court of the Ukrainian SSR.

'This is signed by A. Feldman.† What do you know of his Zionist activities? He's a complete scoundrel (I'm ready to say this to his face) – not only is he getting ready to emigrate himself but he runs around trying to incite others.'

Zhitnikova refused to discuss Feldman.

'Your motives?'

'He's not a scoundrel.'

The Investigator then read from the photocopy of some letter from Israel, which spoke of the bad living conditions the Jews who emigrated from the USSR had to put up with there.‡

(iii) *Her husband's fate depended on her own behaviour.* Investigator Kondratenko produced a photocopy of a statement by T. I. Zhitnikova which had been confiscated during the search mentioned above; at the same time he spoke in an unhurried manner of his understanding

* V. A. Nekipelov was arrested on 11 July 1973, charged with 'disseminating deliberately false and libellous material, defaming the Soviet political and social system'. In May 1974 he was sentenced to two years in labour camp.

† Arrested in October 1973 and later sentenced to 3½ years on a trumped-up charge. *Tr.*

‡ Three or four days after this 'talk', T. I. Zhitnikova received an emigration invitation from Israel, with a July date on it.

of her situation, her wish to make things easier for her husband, to defend him; he said that he himself might have acted in the same way. However, he had to warn her that she had chosen the wrong way to help her husband, that she could be dismissed from her job for that kind of 'help', as she was employed on 'ideological work'.*

'If you had not behaved like this,' he added, 'your husband's fate might have been different.'

What an interesting statement! It turns out that Plyushch ended up in a psychiatric prison not as a result of the legal proceedings carried out by Soviet investigators, the law-courts and the doctors, not because he constituted 'a danger to society', and not even because of his 'state of mental health', but because of T. I. Zhitnikova's behaviour. This had the same kind of logic as the declaration that her letters, statements and appeals to the highest state authorities, asking for a review of her husband's 'case' in accordance with existing Soviet laws – are 'libellous'.

This is the same sort of logic that threatens to deprive a woman who has two children to support, in addition to a husband forcibly committed to a psychiatric prison, of her last crust of bread because of her efforts to restore their father to her children.

Sidorenko, the local Procuracy Investigator, enters. The whole conversation begins again from the beginning.

'Do you still refuse to give evidence?' – and so on, and so on.

Then suddenly a completely incomprehensible question was put to her:

'Comrade Zhitnikova, can you tell us where your children would be looked after during your absence?'

'Why? What absence? I have no intention of leaving home.'

'You see, I can't be sure of anything. In this case I am merely fulfilling the directives of the Moscow Procurator's Office; I have been asked by them to clarify only those points which I have already asked you about.'

'I have my parents.'

And so Zhitnikova began to write letters again. She wrote a complaint to the Procurator's Office of the Ukrainian SSR in

* She worked as a methodologist in the Republic's Methodological Centre for Games, attached to the Ukrainian SSR's Ministry of Education; her job was to approve and report on new games and toys, and to make out methodological recommendations on their use in educational work with children.

Kiev about the illegal seizure from her apartment of her statements and appeals; she protested against the description of these as libellous in the Official Report of the search.

In reply, she received the following letter, dated 4 October 1973:

In answer to your statement I am informing you that L. I. Plyushch has been sent for treatment to a psychiatric hospital on legally justifiable grounds.

As regards your request for the return of your statements, you should apply to the Investigator who confiscated the said documents, concerning this question.

Head of the department in charge of investigations by
State Security organs
Senior Counsellor of Justice
Makarenko

She now returned to the Head of the Dnepropetrovsk Special Psychiatric Hospital (F. K. Pruss) with the following request:

On 22 October this year, when I visited my husband L. I. Plyushch who is at present in your department, I found him in a dangerous state of health – he could not speak and was racked by convulsions (he has never before been subject to this kind of attack).

I was very alarmed by his condition; as he was being given haloperidol, it would be natural to assume his state was due to the influence of this drug.

As far as I know, this drug is usually administered together with a corrector drug, which should alleviate the symptoms produced by haloperidol.

In connection with this, I earnestly ask you to explain to me what kind of treatment my husband is being given, and according to what diagnosis. If the condition I saw him in is produced by haloperidol, is he being given a corrective drug, and if not, why? If you don't possess this medicine, then please explain to me exactly what you need and I shall make every effort to obtain the drugs required.

With respect.

I feel it would be appropriate to quote here an extract from a letter by A. Tverdokhlebov, written in September 1973, in connection with T. I. Zhitnikova's appeal to Comrade V. E. Makagonov, the Head of the Corrective Labour Department Administration (Ukrainian SSR Ministry of the Interior):

The modesty of the request does not do justice to the inner state of the letter's author or that of her husband. Their condition is such that she and her relatives, who know the details of this case, would be justified in coming out into the open and simply shouting for help. But then the last hope would be gone that any of those who have not yet been declared socially dangerous lunatics could somehow help the prisoner of conscience now imprisoned in a special psychiatric hospital [from his letter to Dr Bernard Dixon, published in the journal *New Scientist*, London, 11 October 1973].

I have more than once had the opportunity to see for myself the truth of A. Tverdokhlebov's statement 'Then the last hope will be gone. . . .' I shall give just one example.

At the beginning of August 1973, together with Tatyana Zhitnikova, I had gone to see Judge Dyshel (he presided at the trials of Plyushch, I. Svetlichny, I. Dzyuba, E. Sverstyuk and other dissenters) in order to ask him a question: where was Plyushch being held? Was he still in the investigation prison or had he been transferred to a special psychiatric hospital? If so, which one? Judge Dyshel replied that the Decision of the Court had now been carried out and he was therefore no longer interested in the fate of Plyushch.

'Even if I knew where he was,' he said to Plyushch's wife, 'I would still not tell you, because you wrote a libel about me in your statement to the Supreme Court.'

I asked him to explain what he considered to have been the libel – that the trial was held in closed court, in defiance of the law?

Instead of answering, Judge Dyshel shouted at me:

'As for you, you can just shut up! You're a real counter-revolutionary [*sic*!] and you'll soon find yourself where you ought to be!' He stared at me with hatred, and twisted his hands and wrists to form a peculiar sign, representing a barred window and a lock simultaneously.

'Or even farther away!'

Plyushch's wife has been brought to the verge of despair by her husband's physical and spiritual condition. It is precisely because of this, in spite of threats and searches, that she continues to appear on the doorsteps of Soviet institutions, and goes on writing letters and statements addressed to them.

This is the latest petition that I know she has written:

To the Committee of State Security*
attached to the USSR Council of Ministers.
From Tatyana Ilyinichna Zhitnikova,
    Address: Kiev-147, Enthusiasts St., No. 33, Apartment No. 36

    * The KGB. *Tr.*

Statement

I request you to allow my husband Leonid Ivanovich Plyushch, now in the Dnepropetrovsk Special Psychiatric Hospital YaE-308, to emigrate abroad (together with his family – his wife and two sons).

9.11.73 Zhitnikova

I, for my part, appeal to foreign scientists, writers, artists and especially doctors – to help Leonid Plyushch's wife to obtain permission for the emigration of her husband and their entire family, who have suffered so much.

Forgive me for imposing on you. My strength has run out.

III.3

THE FATE OF LEONID PLYUSHCH SINCE AUTUMN 1973, AS RECORDED IN THE UNOFFICIAL MOSCOW PUBLICATION, *THE CHRONICLE OF CURRENT EVENTS*

From Chronicle *No. 32, 17 July 1974*

On 4 January L. I. Plyushch had his next meeting with his wife. His condition was as before: almost all the time he sleeps; he cannot read or write; he does not go out for exercise as he would freeze. During the meeting he spoke slowly and little, but as previously he listened carefully and with interest; he answered questions briefly.

In February and March the haloperidol treatment was replaced by insulin injections in increasing doses. The team of psychiatrists which examined him at about this time considered it essential to continue Plyushch's treatment. The members of the commission did not speak to Plyushch.

L. A. Chasovskikh, Plyushch's doctor, in response to a question from his wife about which precise symptoms of illness indicated the need to prolong her husband's treatment, answered: 'His views and beliefs'. To further questions about diagnosis and treatment she refused to answer.

At a meeting on 4 March 1974, L. I. Plyushch was unrecognisable. Great dropsical swelling had occurred, he moved with difficulty, and his eyes had lost their usual liveliness.

Plyushch said that the doctors were insisting that he renounce his views and beliefs, and definitely in written form. This he had refused to do.

A commission in April again recommended prolonging Plyushch's stay in the Dnepropetrovsk Hospital. The doctors asked Plyushch to write a detailed autobiography which would show clearly how his views had formed, and how he had developed his 'delusional ideas.' Plyushch refused to write such an autobiography.

At a meeting on 12 May it was learnt that since April they had stopped giving L. I. Plyushch any drugs at all. Plyushch explained this by the fact that pains had developed in his abdominal cavity and the doctors had become scared. With the stopping of the drugs his condition improved: his swellings began to subside, his pains disappeared. Plyushch was transferred to a different ward, where there were fewer patients and it was quieter. He began to read again – true, now only belles lettres, not scientific literature – and to write letters.

At a meeting on 29 May his wife learned that since 13 May her husband had begun again to be given insulin injections, again in increasing doses. Itching and an allergic rash developed, but the injections were not stopped. After each injection Plyushch was tied down to his bed, and it appeared as though by these injections they wanted to achieve an insulin shock.

On the same day (29 May) the commandant of the Dnepropetrovsk Hospital, Pruss, spoke with the wife of L. Plyushch. He said Plyushch still needed treatment and his wife must help the doctors in this regard. 'Your husband reads too much, you must not send him so many books: his sick brain must be spared. You must not forget this.'

In the course of the conversation it became clear that the reading of books in the hospital is strictly controlled and that L. Plyushch was being given very little to read. Letters from those close to him were being taken away as soon as he had read them, and he was not allowed to keep by him even a photograph of his wife and children.

Questions about what drugs Plyushch was being treated with, and in what doses, and whether they were trying to induce in him an insulin shock, were avoided by Pruss and his doctor, who referred to some directives or other, according to which they were not allowed to answer such questions.

At a meeting on 3 July 1974, L. Plyushch reported that in late June he had not been given insulin for 7–8 days, as he had had a cold. However, since 30 June they had recommenced the injections and after 3 or 4 days had again begun giving him a whole syringeful.

L. Plyushch reported that he had been examined by some commission of local doctors. The members of the commission had put three questions to him: 'How do you feel?' 'All right.' 'How does the insulin affect you?' 'It provokes an allergy.' 'How do you regard your former activity?' 'I regret that I got involved in it.'

The commission decided to prolong his treatment.

From Chronicle No. 34, 21 December 1974

In the spring of 1974, mathematicians abroad came to the support of L. I. Plyushch. The Soviet Embassy in Washington has received a petition signed by 650 American mathematicians.

Lipman Bers, a member of the International Committee of Mathematicians for the defence of Plyushch, said in an article published in

Notes of the American Mathematical Society, Vol. 21, No. 6, October 1974, that the petition of 8 July had been returned to the senders. In a letter, signed by V. I. Kuznetsov, Second Secretary at the Embassy, this was said to be because of the petition's 'hostile and libellous character'. Bers writes: 'Mr Kuznetsov did not succeed, however, in pointing out even one inaccuracy in the Committee's statements.'

In August, Academician Sakharov appealed to the International Congress of Mathematicians, which was taking place in Vancouver (Canada), calling on them 'to do all they possibly can to save Leonid Plyushch'.

On 24 August, four members of the Committee for the defence of Plyushch: M. Atya (England), L. Bers (USA), M. Cartan (France) and I. Halperin (Canada) organised a meeting, at which they agreed on the texts of a petition to Kosygin and a telegram to Sakharov. The petition, containing an appeal for the release of L. Plyushch and also asking for his family to be given the opportunity of choosing his form of medical treatment, was signed by 900 delegates at the Congress.

Sakharov did not receive the telegram sent to him on 27 August.

In October 1974, when L. Plyushch was no longer being given insulin, and a new drug had not yet been prescribed, his doctors suggested that he should write a statement condemning his 'anti-Soviet activities' after the manner of Yakir and Krasin. Plyushch categorically refused to do so: 'Yakir lied: do you want me to become a liar as well?' No further suggestions of this kind were made to him and there was no further discussion. Soon a new drug was prescribed for him – triftazine, in tablet form, in large doses.

On 13 November 1974 an external medical commission of experts, led by the head psychiatrist of Dnepropetrovsk District, visited the Dnepropetrovsk Special Psychiatric Hospital. The hospital administration told T. I. Zhitnikova, L. Plyushch's wife, that this commission had been organised because of her activities. Only Plyushch was interviewed by the commission. He was asked three questions:

'How do you feel?'

'Much the same as always.'

'Do you have anything to complain of?'

'I have started to have pains in my chest.'

'What do you know about Valentin Moroz?'

'What a strange question. What can I know of anyone, when I'm completely cut off from the world?'

The Commission decided that it was necessary to continue the forcible medical treatment of Plyushch and to keep on giving him triftazine.

On 15 November 1974 Plyushch was put into a ward 'under surveillance', together with more than twenty aggressive mental patients. The light is never switched off. The patients are not taken outside, even the lavatory is in the ward. From 15 November onwards, Plyushch was given triftazine by injection. The injections of triftazine make him drowsy and inert (but the light makes it difficult to sleep) and also make him shiver constantly. Plyushch does not go for walks (it is not known whether this is because he is not able to do so, or because he is not allowed to). During a scheduled visit, Plyushch hardly said anything and asked no questions, not even about his children. He has almost stopped writing letters: only one letter from him was received last month.

On 16 December 1974 T. Khodorovich, G. Podyapolsky, Y. Orlov (correspondent–member of the Armenian Academy of Sciences), the geologist Malva Landa and the psychologist Boris Landa appealed to 'the Academicians of various countries, and to professional unions of jurists, psychiatrists and journalists':

The torture of mathematician Leonid Ivanovich Plyushch in a special psychiatric 'hospital' is exactly the same kind of revolting crime as the experiments carried out on living people in Hitler's Germany. We appeal to all who prize the human intellect and conscience to defend L. I. Plyushch from further humiliation, by means of protests addressed to the Soviet Government.

On the same day, T. Khodorovich wrote a statement 'to the press, to mathematicians and psychiatrists'. The statement ends with these words:

In the name of common humanity and professional brotherhood, in the name of reason and human rights, in the name of mercy and justice – please HELP Leonid Plyushch and his family to leave the Soviet Union.

On 19 December thirty-eight people made a 'Statement to the Press' calling on the latter 'not to give up, to continue the campaign to free Leonid Plyushch!'

On 20 December T. Khodorovich and Y. Orlov appealed to the 'International Committee of Mathematicians for the Defence of Plyushch':

We call your attention to the danger of establishing the practice of forcible and uncontrolled use of modern drugs in order to "reform" a free intellect and destroy conscience, especially in a very large and powerful country.

We appeal to you to protest to the Ministry of Internal Affairs, the Com-

mittee of State Security (KGB), the Soviet government and the Supreme Soviet, calling for the forcible "treatment" of Leonid Plyushch to be ended at once.
Demand the release of L. Plyushch from a psychiatric prison!

On 20 December 1974, Zhitnikova handed in a statement to the Procurator of Dnepropetrovsk District, asking him to start criminal proceedings against F. K. Pruss, the head of Dnepropetrovsk hospital, Dr L. A. Chasovskikh, head of the hospital's Ninth Department, and E. P. Kamenetskaya, former practising doctor, head of the hospital's 12th Department, on charges of attempting to destroy 'the physical and mental health of L. Plyushch, by means of forcible doses of drugs over a lengthy period, in insanitary conditions'.
On the same day, T. Khodorovich and Y. Orlov sent a statement 'To the International Commission of Jurists, to all professional bodies of psychiatrists', in accordance with a text agreed on by telephone with Zhitnikova:

We appeal to international, independent professional bodies of jurists and psychiatrists, asking them to provide L. Plyushch's wife with a lawyer and a consultant psychiatrist to take part in a legal action she wants to bring against the medical personnel at Dnepropetrovsk Special Psychiatric Hospital . . . L. I. Plyushch's wife asks especially for the participation of the London psychiatrist Gery Low-Beer.

When Zhitnikova, after making a scheduled visit to the hospital, wanted to buy a ticket to Moscow at the Dnepropetrovsk railway station, she was told by the cashier that, although there were seats on the train to Moscow, he regretted that he had been forbidden to sell any tickets, for some reason. Zhitnikova then took a bus from Kiev to Moscow, but the bus was stopped in the suburbs of Kiev by police, and Zhitnikova was forced to get out.
On 27 December 1974 Plyushch's injections were stopped. Because he was no longer under the influence of drugs, Plyushch's health immediately improved somewhat. However, he was not transferred from the 'surveillance' ward.

From Chronicle No. 35, 31 March 1975

In January neuroleptic drugs were again ordered for Plyushch. Again: apathy, indifference, tiredness. Now he wrote only one letter of five or ten lines in a month. He could not read, did not walk.
His wife T. Zhitnikova was refused a second visit in January because

of a quarantine, but she was promised a short meeting a few days later as an exception.

On 4 February the promised meeting did not take place. Hospital director Pruss said that Plyushch had a boil on his face which had begun to swell, and he could not be brought across the yard – 'He might catch cold.'

Between Pruss and Zhitnikova the following dialogue took place:

'Why was Leonid Ivanovich transferred to the high-security ward?'

'In connection with the worsening of his psychic condition.'

'How did this show itself?'

'You complained yourself that he was not writing letters. That was a symptom.'

'But why is he in a ward with violent patients?'

'We are not obliged to tell you where he is being held, or why.'

'Was there a psychiatric commission in January?'

'No. At your request a special commission sat in November, and according to the rules, commissions sit every six months; so now the next will be in May.'

About a week later, despite the continuing quarantine, the meeting none the less took place. Plyushch was in a very bad condition: dropsical swellings had appeared, his apathy had increased, his interest even in his children had vanished. He did not recount anything himself, just answered questions in monosyllables. On his face were red blotches (from erysipelas, according to Plyushch's doctor).

At the meeting on 3 March Leonid Ivanovich looked even worse. To his sleepiness and apathy were added serious dropsical swelling. He was still in the high-security ward, and still taking the same tablets. In the ward he would try to switch off, retreat into himself. This switching-off, already habitual for him, continued even during the meeting. His wife noticed that sometimes his gaze would fade away or would fix itself on something beyond her. At these moments he would neither see nor hear anything. She would have to call out, then he would 'return'. To questions about his health he answered: 'Everything's fine.' A doctor ordered that no books be given him, as 'he already has too many', nor any meat conserves.

Meeting of 21 March: Leonid Plyushch was in the same condition, in the same ward, being 'treated' as before.

Plyushch's doctor L. A. Chasovskikh has been conducting 'health-restoring' conversations with him. She asks L. I. to expound the articles he wrote, which served as material for the charge against him of 'anti-Soviet agitation and propaganda'. She asks him why he wrote them. The doctor tries to instill in her patient the idea that these articles are evidence of his illness, and asks him whether he understands this.

At the meeting Plyushch's wife cautiously hinted to him that, perhaps, he would write a statement which would indicate that he regarded his articles as 'a deviation from the norm'. Plyushch, hitherto apathetic, immediately pulled himself together and said firmly: 'I won't write anything for them.'

At the end of February T. Zhitnikova complained in writing to the Procurator of the Ukraine that the Dnepropetrovsk regional procuracy had not, after two months, replied to her demand to initiate criminal proceedings against doctors of the special psychiatric hospital for giving deliberately wrong treatment (see *Chronicle* 34). In early March she was informed that the Dnepropetrovsk procuracy had been instructed to examine her complaint and reply to it.

On 21 March T. Zhitnikova and T. S. Khodorovich were received by Bedrik, the Dnepropetrovsk regional procurator. He stated that Plyushch's case was a complex one; it was essential that Plyushch be 'examined by professors'; and for his part he 'categorically promised to give a reply in 3–4 days'. However, no answer had come by the end of March.

From Chronicle No. 36, 31 May 1975

The 'medical treatment' of Leonid Plyushch continues:

Leonid Plyushch is still being kept in a surveillance ward and being given triftazine (nine tablets a day). He is still in a serious condition.

In March, T. S. Khodorovich published an article, 'Escalation of Despair'. The article ends: 'How will this crime, sanctioned and initiated by the government, end? It is not difficult to guess? On the one hand, Leonid Ivanovich's bodily health may give out – and that will end with physical death. On the other hand, the barriers of will and spirit, which he has erected in a despairing battle with his executioners, may collapse – and this would result in spiritual death. I take the responsibility of emphasising that both eventualities come to the same thing, that there is little time left, perhaps by now, none at all. A man is not sent into the world to prove his superiority over the products of chemical industry. . . . Leonid Plyushch's wife expects an inevitable catastrophe. There is not one department in the Soviet state machinery to which she can still turn for help, or from which help might be expected.'

On 4 April M. S. Oberemok, procurator of Dnepropetrovsk region, told Tatyana Zhitnikova, the wife of Leonid Plyushch, that her request for a criminal case to be made out against the doctors at Dnepropetrovsk special psychiatric hospital had been refused, as, at the end of March, a medical commission led by Prof. Blokhina (from Dnepropetrovsk) had investigated the medical treatment of Plyushch and the conditions in which he was kept, and had found no infringement of the law. (It later turned out that there had been no commission in March.)

The procurator told Zhitnikova the commission's diagnosis: schizophrenia in its paranoid form. Stating that he knew of the publication of articles on Plyushch in the French press, the procurator advised Zhitnikova to apply 'not to the Western press, but to Soviet institutions. You could be charged with slander!'

On 7 April Zhitnikova sent a letter to A. V. Snezhnevsky, a member of the USSR Medical Academy, who had carried out one of three pre-trial medical examinations on Plyushch. The letter ends as follows: 'I am appealing to the Kiev Regional Court with a request for this forcible medical treatment to be ended, and I ask for your immediate intervention. You are the recognised head of Soviet psychiatry and one of those who produced the diagnosis condemning my husband to indefinite detention in a psychiatric hospital-prison; you bear a heavy moral and professional responsibility for all that has happened. I ask you to stop using nerve-drugs on Leonid Plyushch prior to this court decision: the routine medical commission must see before it a man, not the effect on a man of medical products which have been savagely and inhumanly used on him.'

On 9 April Tatyana Zhitnikova and Yuri Orlov, a member of the Armenian SSR Academy of Sciences, visited the Medical Department of the USSR Ministry of Internal Affairs. In the course of a long conversation, a responsible official of the department said: 'You are acting in the worst interests of Plyushch himself. Would he really be better off being sent to a labour camp?' Zhitnikova requested the Medical Department of the USSR Ministry of Internal Affairs to end the treatment of her husband by means of nerve drugs until the Kiev Regional Court could investigate the question of ending forcible medical treatment and transferring him to another hospital. The same evening, Zhitnikova and Orlov visited A. V. Snezhnevsky at his apartment. During an emotional discussion, Snezhnevsky asked the same question: 'Would it really be better for Plyushch to get seven years of strict-regime imprisonment?' Snezhnevsky promised to ask G. V. Morozov, the Director of the Serbsky Institute, to send his experts to the Dnepropetrovsk special psychiatric hospital immediately.

On 10 April Zhitnikova sent an appeal to the Chief Judge of the Kiev Regional Court, asking for the forcible medical treatment to be ended.

Zhitnikova has not so far received any answer to the letters or to her appeal. The expert commission from the Serbsky Institute, promised by Snezhnevsky, has also not taken place.

23 April was the International Day for the defence of Plyushch. On this day a delegation of five people – two members of the Académie Française, the world-famous mathematicians Henri Cartan and Laurent Schwartz, the lawyer de Félice and two members of Amnesty International, visited the Soviet Embassy in Paris. In the Embassy, those who received the delegation said that 'they would ask Moscow'.

On the same day, T. Zhitnikova's letter was published in the West:

Since the day my husband was arrested, nearly three and half years have passed. Of these he has spent one year in prison, and the rest in the special psychiatric hospital at Dnepropetrovsk. He remembers the prison as a lost paradise: there it was possible to talk and read, and, most important, he was not being 'treated'.

I want to state that the Leonid Plyushch, the 'mathematician Plyushch', as he is called in the broadcasts of Western radio stations, . . . the Leonid Plyushch known to me, to his children, relatives and friends, this Leonid Plyushch no longer exists. Instead there is an exhausted man, driven to the last brink of suffering, losing his memory, and his ability to read, write and think, and terribly ill. And those who with their own hands are killing him know about it – they know they are committing a crime.

There is no 'Plyushch case' – this is a case of human freedom and human worth. If the world grows used to the persecution of free and independent thought, to amorality and complete unlawfulness in actions taken by a government which is responsible for the fate of all humanity, what can we expect from the future? What can we hope for? To what kind of 'tomorrow' are we condemning our children?

Don't think of us, think of yourselves: my terrible 'today' could become the same sort of 'tomorrow' for the great majority of people, if you let your hands fall – if it seems, even for a moment, that your efforts to save reason and conscience are without result.

I did everything to prove his normality . . . his mental healthiness. But now I say: yes, he is ill. Terribly ill, and he needs to be saved from worse than illness, from death.

I have nothing more to hope for in this country. Now all my efforts are directed at getting my application for emigration accepted by the relevant institutions.

. . . I am boundlessly grateful to all the mathematicians abroad, to all who are concerned about Leonid's fate. . . . But I also understand that L. Plyushch's Soviet colleagues have kept silent. They are deaf to injustice, as if the drugs which are suffocating Leonid Ivanovich were also exerting an influence on them.

Let me be given back my husband, ill as they have made him, and let us then be allowed to leave this country. The right to emigration is the only right which I demand to exercise.

On the same day, 23 April, a routine medical commission was interviewing Plyushch (usually these commissions take place in May or June). Nina Nikolayevna Bochkovskaya, in charge of the Ninth Section, told Zhitnikova that the commission had judged it necessary to prolong Plyushch's treatment in a special psychiatric hospital. Bochkovskaya also said, 'Don't worry – we're curing him. He is always under supervision. We're satisfied with his behaviour: he's nice, very polite.' However, when asked about the reasons for Plyushch's confinement in a 'ward for violent patients', she did not reply. The members of the medical commission asked Plyushch only two or three questions: 'What is the effect of triftazine on you? What are you reading? How do you imagine the society of the future?'

Plyushch replied: 'It would be democratic, there should be freedom of conscience, freedom of speech, freedom of the press, democratic elections.'

At the end of April, Leonid Plyushch had meetings with his wife and sister. Plyushch once again had erysipelas (inflammation of the face). His nose had swollen and took up half his face, his temperature was 38·9°. He was being given penicillin injections. He had not been given triftazine for some days. He was in a serious condition. He had forced himself, with difficulty, to attend the meeting with his sister. At the beginning of the meeting, he looked detached, alienated.

At such moments, it seems to the onlooker that Plyushch sees, hears and understands nothing. After some time, his eyes take on a look of comprehension. Leonid begins to answer questions. He answers monotonously and slowly. He volunteers no information, he does not ask about anything. He is limp, inert, indifferent. He is in a depressed state of mind: he has no hope of getting out of the hospital.

Tatyana Zhitnikova was once more informed by the KGB, through a third party, that the methods used in the forcible treatment of her husband depended directly on her own behaviour.

From Chronicle *No. 37, 30 September 1975*

On 15 July 1975 Leonid Plyushch had been held in the Dnepropetrovsk special psychiatric hospital for two years (see *Chronicles* 29, 30, 32, 34–36).

From the beginning of June up to 3 September Plyushch was 'treated' with a combination of drugs: he was given tablets of triftazin and simultaneously injections of insulin. However, they did not, apparently, intend to take things as far as inducing an insulin shock: not once was he strapped to his bed. After 3 September the insulin injections stopped. Triftazin is being administered as before: three tablets at a time, three times a day.

At a meeting in September Plyushch looked bad: swollen, pale, depressed, pessimistic in mood: 'I'm not going to get out of here!'

III.4

MORAL ORIENTATION*

An Essay by Leonid Plyushch

1. *The hare warned the Bear-cub that it was dangerous to go to the river – he might meet with the One who lives in the river. And sure enough, when the Bear-cub glanced into the water, he in fact caught sight of the One who lived in the river. He was frightened but did not let it show, and made a face at the One who lived in the river, a terrible grimace. The other made a terrible grimace in return. Frightened still further, the Bear-cub threatened Him with his paw, but He answered with the same gesture.*

Following the advice of an old Hedgehog, the Bear-cub discovered a way out: he smiled at the One who lived in the river, and that One answered the Bear-cub with a kind and friendly smile.

This parable offers us a remarkably accurate diagram of the development of relationships between a man and his environment, natural as well as social.

The terror of the 'I' before the Other leads to hostile acts against the Other, who answers in kind; this in turn evokes hostility on the part of the 'I' to the Other, and this naturally intensifies the hostility of the Other to the 'I'.

And there is no end to this process, no limit, until the 'I' at last understands that the Other is not reducible to a simple 'not-I', and that to a certain extent the Other *is* 'I', and therefore blows of Another against Me are reflections of my blows against Another.

But that is not all. Without the 'Other' the 'I' ceases to be a reality and turns into an abstraction – it loses not only the shape of its own concrete 'I', but also the sense of any specific 'I'.

Relying on this concept of 'moral orientation', contemporary psychology permits us to elaborate on these old truths.

2. We might define moral orientation as 'a predisposition, the defi-

* Moral orientation, one of several English equivalents of the Russian noun *ustanovka*. Plyushch uses the term *ustanovka* throughout this essay, and it is an expansive, flexible word. 'Orientation', 'setting', 'predisposition', 'set of moral expectations' are all equally appropriate translations in varying contexts. In the technical language of psychology, the word would be translated 'set'; however, this translation seems too technical for the present context. *Tr.*

nite tendency of an organism in certain behavioural situations', a readiness to come to terms with certain definite qualities of the environment during interaction with that environment, the distinctive 'behaviour' of an environment – in short, the expectation of a specific reality.

The behaviour of an individual is determined not only (and even not as much) by the direct influence of the environment, but rather by the moral orientation of the individual in relation to his environment and by the nature of the gap between this orientation and reality.

Uznadze* and his school have shown that this moral orientation permeates the entire activity of the subject, defining the character and direction of his structuring of reality, and also defining his reaction to this reality.

Moral orientation is no less significant in social psychology; in many respects it defines the nature of the interaction between one's own personality and the group, and likewise between group subjects (a social group, a class, a nation and others), influencing the content and development of social consciousness. This influence is felt particularly as regards the origin and consolidation of myths and prejudices (e.g. cf. I. Kon, 'The Psychology of Prejudice', *Novy Mir*, No. 9, 1966).

3. Religious morality is a reflection of already existing relationships between people, fixing and sanctifying these relationships in an idealised form, singling out that which is most generally meaningful. But being a fantasised and idealised reflection of the real, religion offers human society moral orientations which exceed the limits of the past and the present, orientations which play the role of spiritual scaffolding for the future and which influence the direction of social development, thus stimulating feedback in the interaction between 'social existence and social consciousness.

The orientation towards the Good in all world religions may serve as an example of what we are talking about. The formula of zoological justice, 'An eye for an eye, a tooth for a tooth', reflecting the legal requirements of barbarian tribes, underwent moral development in the precept of Judaism, 'Do not do unto your neighbour that which you do not wish done unto you,' and then elevated itself to the new command of Christ, who heralded a future which has still not come to pass: 'And I say unto you, love your neighbour. . . .'

Utopianism, the excessive moral demands of religion, and the dis-

---

* *Dmitry Uznadze* (1886–1950), founder of the school of psychology in Georgia and developer of the psychological theory of the 'set' (see p. 131, fn.).

crepancy between these demands and reality are responsible for the satanic purity and 'perfection' of the first inquisitors, for the religious hypocrisy of the church, and – as a final result and reaction to the above – for the nihilistic amorality of vulgar atheism.

Nevertheless the message of Christ was heard even at the time of the Crusades to the Lord's Tomb and the ferocity of the Muslim Anti-Christ; and as an aim, an ideal, one can hear it in atheistic morality. As an ideal it influences the future and the present, functioning as 'the heart of a heartless world' (Marx).

Vulgar atheism, i.e. a purposeless rejection of religion, sees in religion nothing more than a utopia, and views its social function as an 'opium' which serves to alleviate suffering and therefore also to alleviate man's dissatisfaction with the social order.

Our task consists in this: to preserve all the spiritual values of religion, founding ourselves on social conditions which will do away with the need for spiritual 'anaesthetization'; under such conditions, the same sort of sufferings will have a human character and even possess a certain spiritual value, but they will not be the result of a mechanical pressure from one's social or natural environment.

The existing organization of society is contradictory to the teaching of Christ's disciples – if indeed isolated representatives of this type have really survived, such as the 'holy fools', Don Quixotes and Myshkins (Russian folklore pays tribute to this type in the character of Ivanushka the Fool). Victory comes to these types only as defeat, when their ideals become a dead shell concealing everything with which they have struggled.

Communists have taken stock of the reason for Christianity's defeat, and as a means for achieving the Good they have chosen not personal self-perfection (under present conditions this means is available only to a small group of people, and they survive only because without them society itself could not survive), but rather have chosen to create a society so organized that Christ's orientation or set of expectations for man would not lead to the destruction of Him who bears the message; a society in which that type of man whom we symbolically label Don Quixote or Christ might survive, and for whom love towards his neighbour would not become one uninterrupted heroic deed, the ascent to Golgotha.

The first attempts to create such a society ended in failure, having repeated the victory-defeat pattern of Christ – the ideas were transformed into an idol, into a victim to whom the bearers of these ideas were offered up (it might be added that not only these ideas but all other ideas were demanded as a sacrifice, because idols do not tolerate ideas of any sort, since ideas unmask an idol, exposing the fact that it is dead and can exist only by the blood of living men).

One of the spiritual reasons for this failure was the weakness of a correct moral orientation for good, the predominance of a hatred for Evil over love for the Good – 'the tedious struggle for justice swallows up the love which engendered the struggle' (Camus).

Apparently a struggle for the restructuring of society must be accompanied by a struggle for the restructuring of one's self by means of personal effort. The communist revolution must be accompanied by a Christian revolution, that is, the social must occur with the moral, a Christian revolution must occur in one's own orientation toward Another.

The concept of a good moral orientation by no means presumes that one should love Another regardless of circumstance. Evil does not deserve love; one must hate evil. To Christ alone, an ideal man, was it given to love those who were crucifying him. But to every man is given the potential to elevate himself to Christ.

A good orientation consists in this: to be able to search for an ally, a fellow-human, in Another. This search signifies first of all an opening-up to Another of those areas in oneself which are necessary to him as a fellow-human.

This increases the *probability* of finding and developing an ally for oneself in him. It is a probability only, since the behaviour of Another is not determined by us alone. The Other is himself located in a specific environment, and for him 'I' am only one of the elements in that environment. In order to find the optimal form of interaction with Another, one needs a model of the Other and his environment, that is, a model of My environment, a model which sufficiently accurately reflects reality. A moral orientation towards the good must not substitute a rosy myth for reality, and must not interfere with one's perceptions.

A model of the environment is built on facts. Facts are always insufficient for the conceptualization of a model, however, and it must therefore be completed with the help of various logical, ethical and aesthetic principles (it is therefore possible to speak of logical, ethical and aesthetic orientations).

The same facts are usually simultaneously interpreted as humanistic and anti-humanistic. Consequently the truth in itself does not necessarily negate the good. A striving toward good may become an obstacle on the road to realizing truth, and this can happen even while striving to achieve authentic good if the carriers of good are cowardly and afraid of facts. However the obstacles which a set of moral expectations introduces into the process of cognition are not inherent in these expectations.

Truth-as-justice can point out the path of search for truth-as-objective-truth* while not distorting this objective truth. In the choice between the 'chaos of petty truths' and the 'inspiring deception' we prefer the 'truths', but in an attempt to escape this cruel dilemma we tend to favour the truths that inspire us. This preference might be defined as the primacy of a 'moral orientation towards truth', which on the ethical plane signifies the primacy of authentic justice over the sort of justice alienated from reality in the area of myth: mythological justice.

The problem of the interrelationship between ethics and gnosiology is not settled by the above argument, however. It is also possible for the moral orientation to influence knowledge when the model of reality, formally distorted under the influence of this orientation, in essence reflects reality more deeply, bringing to light possibilities which at first seemed unrealistic and unreal. The 'age paradox' may serve as an example: inexperienced youth cherishes aims which are unrealizable from the point of view of wise old age, yet there are instances when youth achieves its aims. This is explained by the specific character of human perception. The subject, perceiving his environment, changes it in the very act of perception. Therefore those sets of moral expectations lying at the base of his perception can influence the environment, uncovering new possibilities and paths for their realization.

In such a way even the utopianism of a moral orientation may, within known limits, influence the environment in the direction of good – thus are the embryos of future truths hidden in us by the inspiring deception.

4 (a). *Examples of moral orientations: Moral orientation built on the motives of Another*

If the Other has committed an act which is unpleasant to us, then our reaction depends not so much on the action itself as on the predisposition we bring to assessing the results of the action and the motives of the Other as well. If the predisposition is not well intentioned, then the

---

* The Russian term is *istina*, 'holy truth', 'God's truth', an objective reality independent of human interpretation or social justice. *Tr.*

consequences of the act which are detrimental to us will be exaggerated, and we will presume the motives to be negative. There even exists a category of people who enjoy vice, people whom one can only characterize with the label 'baseness of thought'. People with this baseness notice and remember exclusively the negative acts of those closest to them, and coming up against the good, they explain it away with low and selfish motives. A specific example of this base thought is anti-semitic attitudes, or more generally racist attitudes: thinking based on the subconscious or conscious axiom-orientation: 'All the evil in the world comes from the Jews/the Negroes/the Orientals/ etc.'

In Soviet literature the works of Shevtsov and Kochetov* present themselves as brilliant products of such thinking (we are not speaking here of these writers' ideological position – Benyukh and Surkov are almost as reactionary, but their works are free of that pathological relishing of baseness which characterizes the Kochetovs).

The reaction to a negative predisposition can naturally only be negative; it is as if it reinforces the initial predisposition and intensifies it. This phenomenon is a partial instance of a more general rule: *one's set of moral expectations influences reality* (if it influences it at all) *generally in its own direction, drawing reality closer to these expectations.*

Departures from this rule, apparently, are explained by reasons external to the 'I–environment' relationship, for it is not only we who influence the behaviour of the environment. Reacting to the good in Another, I provoke good in him; reacting to the evil in Another, I provoke evil in him as well as in myself.

It follows that the method of analysis of Another's motives given below is the most dignified and the most advantageous from moral as well as pragmatic considerations: in the beginning assume a hypothesis based on good motives, and only later, after experience has refuted this hypothesis, does it make sense to resort to a hypothesis based on evil motives: 'And don't imagine that your act will force us in the future to offer help to people who might be in need of it' (P. G. Grigorenko).

However, reality is complex and situations are possible where a 'good hypothesis' is too risky. In these situations, reality demands first of all that we make provision for evil motives and take the necessary counter-measures. In such a situation, a positive orientation consists in making certain that the counter-measures are of a warning nature only, and do not provoke evil emotions towards the presumed perpetrator of evil.

---

* Contemporary Soviet writers of Stalinist tendency.

4 (b). *Moral orientation in the internal-political struggle*

The history of revolutionary movements shows how quickly comrades-in-arms become enemies. And it is not only objective conditions that are to blame for this.

Continual nervous tension, the abnormal conditions of life, the unnatural interweaving of what is private with what is public all contribute to the important role which personal feuds, sympathies and antipathies play in sharp factional struggle – this is especially noticeable in emigration, in exile, during periods of temporary lull or of shock, when personal relations become the most important thing and the objective crisis of the movement takes on the appearance of personal feuds. With the most self-confident and often most authoritarian revolutionaries, a principle cause of disagreement is their fanatical dedication to principle, which gives rise to an orientation towards *differentiation*, carrying the smallest disagreement to its logical conclusion, changing it into a disagreement of *principle*. And the struggle is often carried on not because of any real dissension but because of some future dissension, a shape which today's difference of opinion *may* assume.

In the final analysis, revolution is bogged down in the blood of the best representatives of all its revolutionary currents, and victory belongs to the 'swamp' which is beyond a current, the 'swamp' led by Bonaparte.

It might be worth while to select from the history of past revolutions examples of this process.

It is especially important at the present time, when the future is barely able to correct the bloody results of the mutual slaughter which goes on between the various currents in the progressive movements.

Therefore the moral orientation of the democratic movement in the USSR must become an orientation towards synthesis, towards union. Naturally this must not occur at the expense of the principles of humanism, freedom and democracy. A synthesis does not mean a mishmash of random details; a synthesis presumes a spectrum of differentiated, clearly reflected opinions, united by a single democratic base. This is particularly necessary and possible for us because we are Soviet reformists, we stand for the evolution of our country and not for armed struggle, which under contemporary conditions is doomed to failure and may provoke a nuclear catastrophe among the super-powers.

On the part of Marxists, atheists and Russians the most important precondition for a union of the various currents is their understanding of the factual inequality existing between other movements and nations, and themselves. The feeling of 'guilt' – even if it is involuntary or 'unreal' – for their proximity to Stalinism, this formal proximity, this understanding of their 'advantages' over other models of democracy ought to help them overcome what is to them a cliché of formal equality among the various relationships and demands people make on each other.

We, Communists, social democrats, must not only search out and support that which we have in common with political democrats fighting for political rights, with religious democrats fighting for the freedom of their convictions, with national democrat-patriots; we must also try to understand their truth to *absorb* and even *appropriate* it, that is, to make it our own truth, to develop it to the level of our own truth even if it is one-sided. A struggle with their ideology as an ideology representing a partial, one-sided humanism must be carried on first of all from the vantage point of their truth.

We will overcome their partiality having overcome our own; overcoming our own incompleteness we will attract to our side all that is close to us, alienating from our allies the reactionary wing of national, religious and political democracy; by the same method we will have developed for ourselves a natural process of internal differentiation between both their and our movements.

If a Russian democrat, confronting the phenomenon of Ukrainian chauvinism, rejects the national problem of the Ukrainians and, even worse, begins to view the entire Ukrainian movement as reactionary, then he will strengthen the chauvinistic wing of that movement and will facilitate a coming-together of chauvinists and patriots.

If our potential allies do not wish to come together with us, then this does not give us the moral right to turn away from their problems – we must make *their* cause *our own*, whether they wish it or not.

We have considered this question of orientation as regards our allies. Naturally one's predisposition towards hostile movements is quite different. It should consist in an attempt to define precisely, in clear ideological and political terms, where they stand in relation to us, and we should expose their anti-humanistic and reactionary essence, if – as is often the case – this essence has a partial democratic veneer.

Using this method, Soloukhin's* signature on a letter defending Solzhenitsyn looks like a political blunder – not only because Soloukhin participated in the persecution of Pasternak.

* *Vladimir Soloukhin*, contemporary Soviet writer with special concern for Russian traditions.

The idea of moral orientation is, however, even more important in the understanding of the enemy. After all, anti-humanism grows in the same authentic soil and feeds on the same reality as does humanism. It is therefore imperative not only to expose anti-humanism in its various reactionary aspects, but also to uncover the deeper causes of anti-humanism's development – that is, to understand its 'truth' and to expose this 'truth' to our truth, in this way depriving the enemy of his sources.

Anti-semitism may serve as a clear example of anti-humanism. Engels defined anti-semitism as 'socialism for fools'. And it was not by chance that the Hitlerites called themselves National-*Socialists*. The fascists seized upon blind national and social protest and directed it against an imaginary enemy. Unfortunately the Comintern ignored this 'socialism' of the fascists, replacing theoretical analysis with generalized phrases and slogans which in the end confused fascism with social-democracy and split the working class. This inevitably led to 'peace and friendship' with fascism.

The same thing is happening today with Maoism – instead of an analysis of the enemy we have curses of every possible variety, and this will lead either to war with China or to 'peace and friendship' with Mao. Under such circumstances it is hard to say which is worse.

4 (c). *Moral orientation in International Relations*

On the international front our movement takes it for granted that the preservation of the world is the basic aim of all foreign policy: the consequent realization of this aim we now demand, and will demand, from our government.

An orientation towards trust between the superpowers is the basis of a peaceful orientation. If the international policy of the USSR is constructed on the basis of presumptions made by the forces for peace in the USA, then we will work to strengthen these forces. If the USSR interprets every proposal of the USA as a provocation, then we will strongly urge the people of the USA to vote for militarism, since no matter what the forces of peace might be, they will bear no fruit – everything will break apart on contact with our lack of trust on principle. A good example is afforded by our refusal to permit mutual inspection as a basis for general disarmament, out of fear of 'espionage' (if we are disarming, then how could mutual espionage threaten anyone?).

An orientation toward mutual trust means giving continual practical witness to peacefulness and trust, and this witnessing alone will lead to the growth of the forces of peace in other countries.

Even the half-way peaceful moral orientation of Khrushchev authentically improved international relations. The war in Vietnam could not but intensify the extremist groups in both blocs. The same could be said about the invasion of Czechoslovakia. The causes of Dr. Spock and [Martin Luther] King will be lost from the start if in the future we continued to decide external political problems by the methods of August 1968.

We must finally understand that a strengthening of reaction in our country automatically provokes anti-democratism over there – just as in its own time the Stalinization of the USSR faciliatated the Hitlerization of Germany. Military hysteria in other countries raises the level of our 'military patriotism'.

In international relations a special place is occupied by nations with an extremist government: in the other camp it is the fascist regimes, in our camp the Maoist–Stalinist regimes. Friendship, mutual aid and unity with them is not sensible (friendship between these extremist governments is more likely, despite their differences in social base). If one of these extremist nations becomes sufficiently strong, war is inevitable. The only solution is the democratization of the superpowers, along with truly selfless, generous and *intelligent* aid to poorly developed nations (totalitarianism grows out of despair!) and a union based on open, international and equitable treaties between the anti-Maoist and anti-Fascist nations – a union which could restrain an aggressor and help the population of aggressive countries find a way out of the blind alley into which history has driven them.

An example of sensible help to poorly developed nations would be anonymous aid (through international organizations) in the areas of education, health insurance, the creation of peaceful industry and raising the productivity of agriculture; this aid would be regulated by the UN in such a manner as to contribute to the democratization and civilization of these nations. At the present time this aid more often pays for the arming of a temporary ally, towards undermining rivals in a given country. Both their side and our own give aid, paying little attention to the fact that we frequently reinforce the power of dictators and juntas.

4 (d).   *Moral orientations toward optimism and pessimism*

An extreme optimistic orientation in one's evaluation of reality is reflected in Pangloss' formula: 'Everything is for the best in this best of all possible worlds.' This sort of optimism permits a man to exist in a state of swinish satisfaction with himself and the surrounding environment. Optimists of such a type serve as the support of any social structure – they see neither the sufferings of those closest to them, nor the atom bomb over their heads, nor the slave bazaars with concentration camps in Siberia. The danger implicit in such a position in our times is sufficiently obvious.

An extreme pessimistic orientation emerges from Pangloss' optimism by the simple substitution of the word 'worst' for the word 'best'. This point of view is perhaps better borne out by the facts, but despite its being throughly contradictory to the optimism of the 'fearless fools' it leads to the same practical behaviour in life – it leads to inertia and an unwillingness to struggle against evil. Therefore the extreme pessimists in their great numbers also become a support for the existing state of affairs, although they are busy creating the illusion of protest.

We might even repeat it again: yes, pessimism is closer to reality, the world is hurtling to its ruin and there is no ray of hope in sight.

But then again, an orientation towards a bad end can only intensify the likelihood of that bad end.

It is possible to escape destruction (if it is possible at all!) only by keeping our eyes wide open while searching for a way out of this blind alley. The struggle to find a way out of the blind alley is possible only if we believe that a way out exists.

As long as there is no certainty that a way out exists, our optimism may rest on the following premise: this entire absurd, tragic-comic pre-history is drawing to a close. We have come to the negation of pre-history, to a negation of the purposeless or the dialectical. We will achieve a good future, or there will be no future at all. A *bad* future, that is a continuation of our dirty and bloody *political* history, will simply not occur.

On this premise one may base one's optimism, which we might call pessimistic optimism: pessimistic because we do not yet see a justification for constructive optimism. The orientation of this optimism is a predisposition to search for possible ways of saving the world, that is, of creating a society which permits a man to become human.

In our view the only other point of view worthy of a man is heroic pessimism – a conviction that the chances for a human continuation of history are negligible, but out of love or respect for myself I 'proclaim my self-will' – I do not want to be a non-entity and I will defend my own human values even should I stand alone.

Unfortunately, such a point of view is suited to isolated individuals only, and cannot become the rallying-point for mass political struggle.
1970

III.5

PRELIMINARY DECLARATION BY LEONID PLYUSHCH AT THE PRESS CONFERENCE HELD IN PARIS, 3 FEBRUARY 1976

I would like to express my gratitude through the press to all those who contributed to my release.

Here in the West: the International Committee of Mathematicians, Amnesty International, the French trade unions, Ukrainian organisations throughout the world; English, French and German psychiatrists, and the Committee against the use of psychiatry for criminal ends in the USSR; and French and Italian communists.

Apart from this, I would like to thank the French government for allowing my family and myself to come to France, and the Fédération de l'Education Nationale (FEN) for material support and help in finding a place for my family in France.

I am especially grateful to my friends in the Soviet Union, who from the first days of my arrest did everytihng possible to bring my case to the notice of people the world over – members of the Initiative Group for the Defence of Human Rights in the USSR. I would like to thank Academician Sakharov personally and those many friends whose names I cannot give, even today.

I would like to thank everyone who has helped my family during these years. The list is very long and includes people in many different countries. I received a great many letters of congratulation which unfortunately it will be physically impossible to reply to. I would like to express my gratitude through the press.

Among all these letters there was only one negative one. It is a curious document and I would like to quote it:

Traitor, degenerate, if they have let you out of Russia for humane reasons then it's a proof that over there there is freedom even for traitors. They acted quite rightly and they were quite justified in putting a lunatic like you in a madhouse. As you weren't in your right mind, you did a lot of vicious harm to your country, scum like you is taken up by the capitalist trusts. They need people like that to keep the workers in bondage. You will dance to their tune, shouting propaganda against your native land. But don't forget this: here too the workers will throw off their yoke. Strikes are springing up all over Europe. Everywhere there are people who are against parasites while defending their own right to life and work. Every worker knows your name. Reproaches apart, you do not deserve the trust of the working people, you came from the people, studied at the expense of the people, it is difficult for the workers here, and this is how you thank the people and the Motherland. May you be damned, you are the dregs of the human race, you and your wife and children. You have soiled your people and your country. Shit must be got rid of, otherwise one falls in it oneself. That's why they kicked you out of a mental asylum and out of Russia. These are the thoughts of the French workers who know that you live in this town.

(The signature was illegible and there was no address.) No comments are necessary. I am sure that a French worker could not write such a letter. It is the point of view of an ordinary Soviet Stalinist. You can see their moral and intellectual level.

I find the sensationalism attached to my name extremely unpleasant. But I hope that it will attract the attention of public opinion everywhere to the plight of dissenters in the Soviet Union and strengthen the fight for human rights all over the world.

Now briefly, something about myself and my 'case'. I am thirty-seven years old, Ukrainian by nationality. I graduated from Kiev State University and am a mathematician by profession. Up till 1968 I worked in the Institute of Cybernetics of the Academy of Sciences of the Ukrainian Republic. Officially I was dismissed because of a reduction in staff, but in fact it was because of a letter of protest sent to *Komsomolskaya Pravda* about the Ginzburg–Galanskov case. After that I was unable to find any work. In January 1972 I was arrested and accused of anti-Soviet propaganda.

Why was I sent to prison and then to a mental hospital?

In 1964 after the fall of Khrushchev I wrote a letter to the Central Committee of the Communst Party in which I developed my ideas about the democratization of the Soviet Union. By chance the letter got into the hands of the KGB. The KGB talked to me and asked me to refrain from writing any such lettters for (for some reason) two years. I kept my job and even continued as a political teacher, running a philosophy seminar.

From 1966 on I began to write articles for *samizdat*. The articles were about the nature of the Soviet state and its ideology and about the problems of the nationalities in the USSR. A convinced Marxist,

I based my examination of these questions on the works of Marx and Lenin. I proved that Stalinism represented a Thermidorian Bonapartist degeneration of the October Revolution, that state capitalism had been built in the Soviet Union, that property belonged to a state which was alienated from all classes, that property did not belong to the people, and that the bureaucracy is the servant of an abstract type of capitalist – the state. As far as the nationalities are concerned, the Soviet Union is continuing the policy of the tsarist government.

I considered that revolution in the Soviet Union was impossible and undesirable; what was absolutely necessary was a gradual democratization of the country through reforms from above and the propagation of democratic ideas among the people. Wishing to be of some practical help in the struggle for democratisation I circulated *samizdat*, collected information for the *Chronicle of Current Events* and the *Ukrainian Herald*, which were both documenting the struggle for human rights in the USSR.

In 1969 I became a member of the Initiative Group for the Defence of Human Rights in the Soviet Union, which legally protested against infringements of the Soviet Constitution and the Declaration of Human Rights.

On 15 January 1972 I was arrested and put in an investigation prison of the KGB in Kiev. I was charged with everything described above. From the first day of the investigation I refused to make any statement whatever. I knew that anything I said about my friends even if it was in their favour, would only be used for some charge against them. Neither the KGB nor the Procurator's Office was interested in the truth. I told the investigators that I considered the KGB an anticonstitutional organisation and that I did not wish to be a party to their crimes against the people.

As early as 1969, an acquaintance of mine, Bakhtiyarov, was told during an investigation that I was a schizophrenic and that I was in a mental hospital. For this reason I was convinced from the first day of my arrest that I would be put in the Dnepropetrovsk mental hospital. I realized that my tactics of silence during the investigation increased the threat, but I did not want to go against my principles.

In May 1972 I was sent to the Serbsky Institute for a so-called in-patient forensic psychiatric examination. But for 6 months I was held in Moscow's Lefortovo Prison. The decision to send me for compulsory treatment was taken on the ground of several conversations with psychiatrists, among whom were some leading figures in Soviet psychiatry – Academician Snezhnevsky, Lunts, Nadzharov and the Morozovs. I went before two psychiatric commissions. As I subsequently found out the diagnosis was 'sluggish schizophrenia from an early age'.

From July 1973 to January 1976 I was in the Dnepropetrovsk special mental hospital. I underwent 'treatment' by neuroleptics – haloperidol and triftazin – and I was given two courses of insulin therapy.

Most of the inhabitants of the Dnepropetrovsk special mental hospital are mentally deranged – murderers, rapists, hooligans. There are about sixty political prisoners, in general mentally normal people. These are people like Plakhotnyuk,* Yatsenko, Ruban, Evdokimov and Lupinos, who are there because of so-called 'anti-Soviet activity', and also people who have tried to leave the USSR for the West – 'the border-crossers'.

The horror of a *psikhushka* (mad house) gripped me from the start. In the ward there were more patients than beds. I was put as the third person on two bunks that had been pushed together. On the beds patients were writhing from haloperidol. One man's tongue was lolling out, another man was rolling his eyes, a third walked around unnaturally bent over. Some lay and groaned with the pain – they had been given injections of sulphur. As they explained to me, they were being punished for bad behaviour.

All the patients walked around in their underclothes, which were without buttons. I felt embarrassed in front of the nurses, as one's genitals were visible in these 'clothes'. Patients stood around the door and begged the orderlies to let them go to the lavatory.

When I woke up next morning, I saw two orderlies beating up a patient. In the afternoon I was summoned for interrogation by Dr. Kamenetskaya. An orderly came in and said that a patient had attacked some orderlies and had then tried to hang himself in the lavatory. The doctor ordered him to be tied up, and burst into the ward and started shouting at him.

The patients told me that he hadn't attacked anyone, but he had been beaten up because he had asked to go to the lavatory. But no one could make up his mind to tell a doctor about this because they were afraid of being punished with sulphur. The patients began to make

* Dr. Mykola Plakhotnyuk, a Ukrainian born in 1936, arrested in 1972 for his *samizdat* activity.

fun of the victim, but he told them: 'They'll beat you up too, you know.'

I had arrived at the prison with a group of thieves, who were feigning illness in order to 'have a rest' and a good feed. On the second day they all admitted that they were quite healthy – they were horrified by what they had seen.

A week later I was taken to another floor. Here the regulations were not so strict – hardly anyone was writhing in pain from haloperidol; it was easy to get to the lavatory, the patients wore dirty, ragged clothes; but they were pyjamas. . . .

They put me on a plank bunk between two patients – one man was seriously ill and had completely lost any resemblance to a human being (he was swollen, defecated where he lay and spent his time masturbating). As he was dying he was soon transferred to an ordinary hospital. This is a common practice designed to bring down the death statistics.

The political prisoners immediately explained to me that you shouldn't complain here. If you did you were given intensified treatment with neuroleptics and injections of sulphur, and they prevented you from going to the lavatory.

You had to admit to the doctors that you were ill and renounce your views. At the beginning I argued with them, but then I came to the conclusion that they were right.

I met a journalist from Leningrad called Evdokimov, a member of the NTS.* We began to have ideological arguments. They broke us up, saying we were *antisovietchiki*. One of the orderlies told the patients we were 'yids'. Several patients began to complain that we prevented them from sleeping during the day. I was put in another ward. There was a political prisoner there as well. But the doctors warned him not to speak to me. He didn't.

One very sick patient who was known as 'Mister' used to yell out anti-Soviet slogans and asked me to correct his delirious letters to the Soviet authorities. The orderlies promised to 'smuggle them out' secretly and in return took all his food parcels from outside. He died after two months.

The orderlies in the hospitals are criminals serving out their sentences. They demand groceries, socks, etc., from the patients, in return for

---

* Usual translation is 'Popular Labour Alliance', a Russian anti-Soviet émigré organisation based in Frankfurt and Paris.

which they allow you an extra visit to the lavatory or increase your ration of tobacco. If you refused to give them the bribe they might beat you up. They beat Evdokimov up for this. I complained to the doctor and things got worse. They searched me several times a day and took away my tobacco. I had to give them the bribes.

According to the rules they take you to the lavatories in groups six times a day and during three of the visits you are allowed to smoke. The patients try to smoke as much as they possibly can, and as a result often vomit.

I was prescribed haloperidol in small doses. I became drowsy and apathetic. It became difficult to read books. I started to secretly spit out tablets.

After three months they put me in the worst department – No. 9. Here the arbitrary rule of the orderlies is less evident, but to make up for it the 'treatment' is much more intense. You are under more strict supervision and the doctor's interrogation becomes more humiliating.

I was put in a so-called 'supervised ward' where they put the serious violent cases – some fight, others writhe in epileptic fits, one cries, another roars with laughter, another sings thieves' songs, another describes his case and his sexual adventures in a loud voice, another asks to go to the lavatory – in short, bedlam.

Then one of the 'border-crossers' asks to go to the lavatory. He is incontinent and has the doctor's permission to go at any time. But the orderlies do not take this into account, so he urinates on the floor in the ward. He is not the only one who uses this form of protest. . . .

In the lavatories the picture is even more depressing – it is full of people, there's a fight for a place at the 'peep-hole' people search for cigarette stubs among the used lavatory paper. Some of the patients also eat their excrement or masturbate. I don't want to blacken the picture – this last did not happen every day.

I was considered the most dangerous patient in the hospital. The orderlies and nurses were forbidden to talk to me. The other political prisoners were warned that if they talked to me it would be the worse for them. When one orderly started to take science fiction books from me he was told that he was associating with an *antisovietchik*. For two days I sat next to a political prisoner in the dining-room, but they moved us to different tables.

Once I talked to a young murderer for a whole evening – about science fiction. The next day he was put in another ward. What is more, the doctors reproached me for making friends with another murderer, which was completely untrue. At the same time they reproached me for not talking to any of the patients. To keep me in complete isolation I was forbidden to go to the kitchen or into the yard in case I might accidentally meet other politicals.

Even eight months before my trial, instructions were given to the Dnepropetrovsk prison that I was not to have any contact whatsoever with the doctor from Kiev, Plakhotnyuk.

At the interviews, the doctors asked me about my contacts outside. I told them that these questions were interrogator's questions and refused to answer them. The interviews themselves were very painful for me as they discussed my beliefs and made humiliating comments about them. They commented on my letters and the letters to my relatives. When my wife complained about something in the behaviour of my elder son and praised the younger son, they told me that the elder was on the right track whereas the younger was schizophrenic. They hinted that my wife wasn't normal either. And as for a close woman friend who wrote me affectionate letters, she was supposed to be my mistress and so they would not give me her letters.

In general the doctors suggested I cease writing to all my friends as they were all *antisovietchiki* and my correspondence with them proved that on leaving the hospital I would continue my 'anti-Soviet activities'.

After the Yakir–Krasin trial they suggested I write a confession. I asked them, 'Do you really think that an adult can change his views so quickly? They must be lying.'* The doctor agreed that they lied but continued to put pressure on me to recant.

But a confession was not enough; there had to be proof that it was genuine, and there had to be proof why I considered I was mentally ill. I answered the last question carefully, saying that I was not a specialist and that I could not express an opinion about my own illness. Here it must be taken into account that I did not know their diagnosis and did not know what I should be disputing.

A few words about doctors – their moral and intellectual level.
A patient: When will I be let out?
Doctor: Not until I'm on a pension.

---

* Yakir and Krasin were two Soviet dissenters arrested in 1972. After some months in prison they were induced to recant and give the KGB extensive information about their fellow-dissenters.

One of the patients called the doctors Gestapo–ists. They prescribed injections of sulphur. (After an injection of sulphur your temperature goes up to 40°, the place where you had the injection is very painful, you cannot get away from the pain. Many people get haemorrhoids as a result of sulphur injections.) This patient groaned loudly for twenty-four hours. Mad with pain, he tried to hide himself under the bed; in despair he broke the window and tried to cut his throat with the glass. Then he was punished again and beaten up. He kept asking everyone: 'Am I going to die?' and only when he really did begin to die, and another patient noticed it, did they stop the sulphur. And for two days they gave him oxygen and brought him various medicines. They saved him. As I understood, the use of sulphur was counter-indicated for him.

In a nearby section a patient, a common-law criminal, told the doctors that three political prisoners (one of whom was dumb) 'are having anti-Soviet conversations'. These patients were suspected of plotting. When they searched the dumb one they found a note: 'And how much do oranges cost?' This was regarded as a coded message. They began to inject into the veins of the 'conspirators' doses of barbamyl hitherto unheard-of in the hospital. They were brought into the ward completely unconscious. At the same time they began to give them sulphur, without any explanation. And then we heard about the 'conspiracy' in a roundabout way.

Dr. E. N. Kamenetskaya, whom the patients called Ilse Koch,* boasted in front of Evdokimov that she had bought Remarque. He gave her the nickname 'Remarque'. Someone reported the nickname, and Evdokimov was then put on haloperidol.

Doctor Lyubarskaya† said to me: 'You are just an ordinary person – why did you go in for politics?' I explain that one of the ideas of the communists was the involvement of all working people in political activity. The Bolsheviks were ordinary people too. Answer: 'But you're not a Bolshevik', and she goes on to explain:'Your abnormality is shown by the way you have always from an early age been concerned with things that were none of your business' (she was thinking of my activities at school when I took part in the Brigade which helped the border guards; then I was in the vigilantes who went after thieves, speculators and prostitutes – that is, I was an active Komsomol member).

* Name of a notorious Nazi extermination-camp doctor.

† Dr. L. A. Lyubarskaya is mistakenly called L. A. Chasovskikh in the *Chronicle* and some other sources.

The following episode says a great deal about the professional standard of the doctors. I asked the same doctor: 'Why is psychotherapy not used in the hospital?' Answer: 'There is no use for psychotherapy in psychiatry.'

I have described what I heard and saw. But I was asked to describe what it was like before I was there.

The conditions for both the sick patients and the sane ones were much worse. The orderlies used to beat them up for the slightest thing, and they nearly beat them to death.

The doctor in charge of my case, Dr. Lyubarskaya, was the head of a department. In her department the orderlies killed a patient. The incident was hushed up and the orderlies were sent off to a camp. Lyubarskaya was transferred to our department as a simple doctor.

At the beginning of the 1970s the male nurses destroyed the liver of a political prisoner called Grigoriev by beating, and he died. Obviously such incidents led to 'a relaxation in the regulations'. I cannot check these stories, but I heard about this from political prisoners whose sanity I do not doubt and from ordinary criminals.

To sum up – what is the aim of such 'treatment' and regulations? I saw in my own case that the first days are meant to break a person morally straight away, break down his will to fight. Then begins the 'treatment' with neuroleptics. I was horrified to see how I deteriorated intellectually, morally and emotionally from day to day. My interest in political problems quickly disappeared, then my interest in scientific problems, and then my interest in my wife and children. This was replaced by fear for my wife and children. My speech became jerky and abrupt. My memory also deteriorated.

At first I felt it keenly when I saw the patients' suffering or learned that some friends had turned traitor. Then I became indifferent to it. The effect of the neuroleptics increased my isolation from the healthy politicals. I did not want to hear the cries, the fights, the laughter, the crying, the delirium. For whole days on end I lay and tried to sleep. The neuroleptics helped me.

I did not have a thought in my head. The only thoughts that remained were – the lavatory, smoking and the 'bribes' you had to give to the orderlies to get an extra visit to the lavatory, And one other thought – that I must remember everything I saw there, so I could describe it later. Alas, I didn't remember a hundredth part of what I saw.

In spite of my apathy I was afraid that my deterioration was irreversible. I looked at the really serious cases who, they told me, had been quite well a few years ago: one had been able to communicate with them. Several politicals broke down and gave up before my eyes. I was very worried by the physical health of Evdokimov and Plakhotnyuk. I must emphasize that thanks to the protests of my wife and friends and the concern expressed by public opinion in the West great attention was paid to my physical health. The same cannot be said of the others.

I consider my statement and this press conference as an opportunity to draw the attention of public opinion all over the world to the situation of political prisoners in the USSR and to call upon people everywhere to intensify their fight for human rights throughout the world.

Being a communist by conviction, I would like to address myself to communists in the West. When I was in Dnepropetrovsk special mental hospital I found that among those fighting for my release were French and Italian communists. I did not think that this would help me personally. It was the fact that they were taking part which made me glad – for me it meant that these communists were fighting for a humane socialism.

We Soviet neo-Marxists have always hoped that the Italian, French and English communist parties will carry on the work of the Czecho-slovak Communist Party and will rehabilitate communist ideals and put the CPSU in the position of having to choose between Mao-Stalinism and communism with a human face.

I hope that these parties will take an active part in the struggle to find a way out of the deadlock in which all mankind now finds itself – in 'socialist' and capitalist countries alike.

Here in the West, I consider it a duty to my conscience to join in the fight for the release of political prisoners from the prisons, camps and psychiatric prisons of the USSR. At the moment the fight is going on for the release of my friends Vladimir Bukovsky, Semyon Gluzman and Valentin Moroz. I call on all honest people to join in this fight.